BELIEVE

BELIEVE

The Autobiography

Oleksandr Zinchenko

with Raphael Honigstein

BLOOMSBURY PUBLISHING
LONDON · OXFORD · NEW YORK · NEW DELHI · SYDNEY

BLOOMSBURY PUBLISHING
Bloomsbury Publishing Plc
50 Bedford Square, London, WC1B 3DP, UK
29 Earlsfort Terrace, Dublin 2, Ireland

BLOOMSBURY, BLOOMSBURY PUBLISHING and the Diana logo are
trademarks of Bloomsbury Publishing Plc

First published in Great Britain, 2024

Copyright © Oleksandr Zinchenko, 2024

Oleksandr Zinchenko is identified as the author of this work in accordance
with the Copyright, Designs and Patents Act 1988

Photographs are from the author's personal collection except
where credited otherwise

All rights reserved. No part of this publication may be reproduced or
transmitted in any form or by any means, electronic or mechanical, including
photocopying, recording, or any information storage or retrieval system,
without prior permission in writing from the publishers

A catalogue record for this book is available from the British Library

ISBN: HB: 978-1-5266-7469-2; TPB: 978-1-5266-7605-4; EBOOK: 978-1-5266-7468-5;
EPDF: 978-1-5266-7467-8; WATERSTONES EXCLUSIVE: 978-1-5266-8516-2

2 4 6 8 10 9 7 5 3 1

Typeset by Newgen KnowledgeWorks Pvt. Ltd., Chennai, India
Printed and bound in Great Britain by CPI Group (UK) Ltd, Croydon CR0 4YY

MIX
Paper | Supporting
responsible forestry
FSC® C171272

To find out more about our authors and books visit www.bloomsbury.com
and sign up for our newsletters

To my mum, who gave her all to make my dream happen.

To my dad, who taught me so many things.

To my stepdad, who showed me the importance of working hard always.

To my beautiful wife, who is my inspiration and soulmate.

To my daughters, who are my life and the biggest motivation imaginable.

CONTENTS

1. Ball, Ball, Ball ... 1
2. The Big Freeze ... 15
3. Catching a Break ... 33
4. In But Out ... 53
5. From Zero to 100 ... 73
6. Treble Winners ... 103
7. Cracking the Code of Football ... 123
8. Porto Blues ... 143
9. Into the Darkness ... 155
10. North London Calling ... 169
11. Gold ... 187
12. The Wrong Side of Poznan ... 213
13. United for Ukraine ... 227
14. Chasing Perfection ... 241
15. Believe ... 263

Acknowledgements ... 276
Image Credits ... 277

1

Ball, Ball, Ball

'Why are you crying, Alex?'
'No one passes the ball to me.'
'You better get it yourself then.'

I've had these words etched into my head for over 20 years. It's the most important thing my mother ever taught me about football. And life.

Don't wait for it. Make it happen.

I was seven and the youngest player on my local team, Karpatia Radomyshl. There was only one age group under 11. Everyone else was much taller, stronger, better. I didn't have a team shirt either – I was too young to get a squad number. My mum bought me a normal red top in a shop so I could at least wear the same colour as everyone else. But it didn't quite look right and neither did I. Playing in the courtyard outside our apartment building with my friends, I was quite good. This was real football though, with corner flags, goal nets and everything. My new team-mates took one look at this primary school kid half their size and decided to ignore me completely. What was I doing there? I went home from my first day sobbing.

But that wasn't end, only the beginning. A few days later, we went to play a tournament in Skadovsk, a city on the Black Sea, around a thousand kilometres away. My mother was one of the parents that accompanied the team, and she watched all the games. But when I finally came on, she was not there to see me. She had gone to a shop to buy something. She got back after a few minutes and asked for the score. 'One-nil,' one of the other parents told her. 'And your boy has scored the goal.'

'Impossible,' she replied, convinced it was some kind of joke. She couldn't believe her little kid could do that. And yet it was true. The manager had put me on as a striker, and I scored.

It was only a goal in a provincial youth tournament, against opposition I cannot remember, and the result was of no consequence at all. But it might just be the most important goal I ever scored. From that moment on, my mum understood I was too committed to stop, that I would give everything to be a footballer. After Skadovsk, she was all-in. Without her help, devotion and sacrifice, you wouldn't be reading these words today.

Radomyshl, my birthplace, is a small town two hours west of Kyiv. It felt more like a village. Not a poor place, but definitely not wealthy either. There weren't any rich people there. If someone had a bit more money than others, you'd never see it. Everyone lived in the same kind of apartment in the same kind of blocks. Standard USSR issue, no frills.

My father was a builder who travelled a lot for work. Having a dad who's hardly at home was quite tough, but it made every moment we spent together very special. He loves football, like me, and texts me after every game with his thoughts. In his youth, he played for Karpatia as well, but someone broke his leg. He needed surgery and never played again in a team.

My mother sold food, including bread and other basic provisions, first in a market, then a little shop. Later, she worked in an office, providing secretarial services for people who needed to print a letter or copy documents. We didn't have tons of money, but my parents worked hard to give me a great life. They saved for us to go to the Black Sea on holiday once a year and gave me a taste of that healthy sea air. I never wanted for anything. Radomyshl had one supermarket, one disco. In those days, I was too young to go and only ever once visited when I came back years later. I can't say I enjoyed it very much. Loud music and drinking is not my thing. I much prefer going to a restaurant with friends and having a conversation. There was also a cinema that stood empty for a long time. I saw one film there: *Finding Nemo*. It's a story about a child getting separated from his family and having to fend for himself in a hostile environment…

Kids had lots of time on their hands but few options. In those days, nobody had any digital devices. We went for a swim in the nearby pond. We played tag. We played hide-and-seek. We rang the doorbells outside apartment blocks and ran away. We played football on a pitch outside our house that had a pull-up bar near the bins for one goal and a big boulder for the other. We drew a goalkeeper on it.

On one side of our little field of dreams was a bit of sand, on the other, a pavement, and the shape of the pitch was like one of those Tetris pieces that has one bit on the top left, two in the middle and one bit on the lower right. You literally couldn't see one goal from the other. After a couple of years, we had to move to a different street because somebody built a pub where the bins used to be.

Winter was the best, when everything was covered with snow. You could make sliding tackles then. Sliding tackles on snow is the absolute best. I actually feel a little sorry for myself that I signed with an academy at 11 and didn't play street football – especially in winter – for a few more years. It's the best fun I ever had. I would have liked to enjoy that for a little longer.

Balls were at a premium because they got destroyed all the time. You'd hit a sharp corner or a stone on the ground, and bang, they were gone. Whenever my parents asked me for a present, 'ball, ball, ball' was all I said. But I also got a Ronaldinho shirt once. Not a real one, of course: a knock-off from the local market. The quality was not the greatest, but it came with the big '10' on the back and his name, which was all that mattered to me. He was my favourite player, my absolute idol. My room was plastered with posters of him. It was a shrine. I also had a

Steven Gerrard Liverpool top but didn't wear it as much. Ronaldinho was the one for me.

We lived in an apartment with five floors and similar buildings nearby, so there were always enough football players around for spontaneous games. We used to stage our own tournaments. One building against another, young vs old, white T-shirts against coloured T-shirts. I was often the youngest, which meant I had to play a bit differently. I couldn't rely on physical strength to get out of trouble or to win the ball. My decision-making had to be better, which is to say, I had to think one or two steps ahead of my opponent. If you pass the ball quicker or move into space quicker than him, the fact that he's bigger matters a lot less.

At Karpatia, I started playing as a striker, dropping into midfield, 'a false 9' in modern terms. I scored a lot of goals. The older I got, the further I was moved back by the coaches, probably because they saw where my way of playing was making the biggest difference to a team. I was worried I'd end up as goalkeeper one day, but I would have played there happily, too.

I'm an only child, but my cousin lived close by and we played a lot together. He was like a brother to me. But I couldn't say what we did in any great detail. Painting? Toys? I don't remember any of it; my mind is blank. It was only football for me. Honestly, I was obsessed. We trained twice a week with Karpatia, Tuesday and Thursday, outside in the summer. Inside, with a futsal ball, in winter. The days between and before the next game were agony for me. I couldn't handle not playing.

Aged eight or nine, I once told my mum, 'Do anything you want to punish me. I don't mind standing in a corner for hours. But you cannot take away football from me. Never, in your life, tell me I can't go to a training session.' At that point she knew this was real. She could see it in my eyes. This guy was not going to stop. The game was a sickness for me.

I smashed a lot of windows in my school, kicking the ball between lessons. My parents weren't happy, but they understood there was no cure. And I was so afraid they'd put a stop to me playing that I was otherwise the perfect boy. I never got into any real trouble. I never smoked. I never drank. My grades were good. One was the worst and 12 was the best, but none of them was lower than a ten for me. I never once skipped class. I regret it a bit now because it would have been fun, going off on an adventure while everyone else was doing maths. But no, that's not where my head was at. Or should I say: my feet.

One day, I was 11 at the time, we played against one of the neighbouring villages and I was noticed. My coach told me that one of the coaches who worked at an academy had seen me play and wanted to invite me for an open-day trial. I had no idea what an academy was. He explained that it was a boarding school for footballers. Talented youngsters went there to live and learn to play the game. That got my attention.

'One small thing though,' he said. The open day was for kids born in 1995. I was born on 15 December 1996. They would be at least one year older than me, and if they were born in early 1995, nearly two. It was quite a difference at that age. But that didn't worry me at all. I was used to playing with boys from 1992 and sometimes even bigger guys than that. '1995? Perfect. When do we go?'

It wasn't that straightforward. The academy was called Monolit and located in Chornomorsk, on the Black Sea, 540 kilometres to the south. The travel alone cost a lot of money, to say nothing about accommodation and so on. My coach thought I might also have an opportunity to get a trial at Dynamo Kyiv, who were less than a couple of hours away. That would have been much easier. Dad and my uncle drove there to make enquiries and came back with bad news. They wouldn't look at anyone younger than 14. No exceptions.

My parents were determined I should be given that chance at Monolit. They saved up money and took me by bus. I think it took about ten hours to get there. Monolit had an artificial pitch the size of which I had never seen. We played five vs five at Karpatia on artificial grass, and the seniors had a full-size grass pitch. But a full-size artificial pitch? Wow. I couldn't wait to get on it. The coach who met us said: 'You are lucky. We have two games today.' Two games after a ten-hour bus journey? Okay. I had so much energy as a child. I didn't need to warm up.

The staff later told me that they didn't take me seriously at first. I was only 11 and everyone else was 12 or 13, decent talents from that age group from all over Ukraine. But they could see that I could play a bit. I wasn't shy on the pitch either. I played the first game as a left midfielder, scoring some goals and making a few nice assists. I played the second game as a striker and scored more goals. I was used to playing against real teenagers at Karpatia. Here, everyone was older, but not by that much. It felt so easy by comparison. And the players at the trial were of a really high standard, technically. They understood the game. Playing up front with them was a pleasure, because they knew how to find you with their passes.

The head coach was happy with what he saw. He asked me to stay for the night and play a bit more the next day. But then the doubts set in.

I shared a room with two boys. One of them, a big guy, a central defender, was really homesick. He couldn't take the idea of being away from his parents. He called his mum from a phone in the hallway and cried bitterly into the receiver. 'Please, Mum. Take me home. I can't stay here. You have to take me,' and so on. Seeing this boy, one year older than me, having a meltdown suddenly got me very scared. Living all alone far from my family, with boys I had never met before, at a new school… If he couldn't take it, how could I?

My mum and dad were staying in a nearby hotel for the night. I called them and begged to be taken back home. 'Please, Mum. It's too hard here. I want to go.'

She arrived the next day and tried to talk me round. 'Alex,' she reminded me, 'you always had a dream to be a footballer. This is your chance and you have to use it. This is an incredible place that will help you fulfil your potential.' I heard her, but she couldn't alleviate my fears. The head coach tried his luck, too. 'Alex,' he said, 'this is the place for you. You need to be here.' When he saw that there was no getting through to me, he changed tack. 'You know what we'll do?' he said. 'Go home for three days. Think it over, and then please give us a call. Because we need you back.'

Smart move.

After three days in Radomyshl, I knew I couldn't say no to this opportunity. I went back to Monolit, to a new life and a new school. All my life, I had learned in Ukrainian, but in the south, they spoke Russian in school. It took me about two months to get used to it. The language was different, but I didn't feel like an outsider because of that. Everyone felt Ukrainian. Part of Russia's excuse for invading in 2022 was that our country was forcing Russian speakers to talk only Ukrainian. It was a barefaced lie, one of many. In 18 years of my life there, no one ever forced me to speak Ukrainian.

It was normal for both languages to be spoken there. Many spoke Russian, because that had been the official language when they grew up as part of the Soviet Union until 1991. It's very easy for most Ukrainians to understand Russian as a result, but Russian speakers understand Ukrainian less readily. After my move to Monolit, I mostly spoke Russian with the people around me. The moment the February 2022 invasion happened though, I was so angry that I vowed never to speak Russian again. It's been only Ukrainian since.

The regime at Monolit was ultra-professional. At 5.30, the alarm went. I prepared my kit and put it under the bed to save myself a few minutes in the morning. We had a training session before school, then another in the afternoon, then dinner, then we would play on one of the pitches outside the academy until the sun set. Kicking the ball all day, I grew quite a lot.

Morning sessions focused on technique. There were a lot of repetitions: control the ball with the outside of your foot, with the inside. You do it so often so you don't have to think about it; it happens automatically. Like when you're walking a few metres, you don't have to tell your legs, left, right, left again… You think about it and it happens. With good football technique, drilled into you from an early age, it's the same. The better your basics, the sooner you can concentrate on other things, like your opponents or where your team-mates are.

As one of the shorter boys, I had to do a lot of jumping in those morning sessions. Academies use a contraption called a pendulum header – a ball attached to a rope and a stick – to teach this skill, but at Monolit the coaches showed us a tree at the training ground. 'Jump and touch one of the leaves with your head.' I took one look and thought they were out of their minds. Impossible. But within a week, I could do it. I must have jumped under that tree a thousand times. That's the reason my heading is quite decent these days for a guy of my size.

I spent only one and a half years at Monolit, but it felt like five because there was so much football and the drills were so intense. In my opinion, every young footballer would benefit from receiving a similar education because, in those early teenage years, you can still improve the foundations a lot.

Physically, it was not always easy though, because I trained with the Under-13s. There was one long-distance test where we had to run three kilometres in 12 minutes. With a few laps left, I was totally out of energy and told the coaches I couldn't go on. As I was the youngest in the group, they said it was fine for me to stop, but I thought to myself, 'No, it really isn't.' I tapped into my last reserves and managed to finish with the race leaders.

I had a dream one day that I missed training, but I didn't realise it was only a dream after I woke in the middle of the night. I threw on my kit as quickly as I could and stormed out in a panic, looking to find my team-mates. There was no one there. Could they have gone to an away game? I decided the best I could do was a few laps and hope to meet someone. The team and coaches arrived half an hour later, wondering what I was doing out so early. I was too embarrassed to tell them the truth and said I had gone out for a walk, but I don't think they bought it.

A year or so later, I was actually late. I had dislocated my elbow and took a bit longer to change into my school clothes after training. Viktor, one of the coaches, asked the school bus to wait an extra five minutes for me, but they ran such a tight schedule that the academy director refused the request. They left without me. I had no choice but to run to school with my damaged arm. Luckily, the school was only three or four kilometres away, so I nearly arrived in time.

On Sundays we had a day off but mostly spent it in the academy grounds, playing more sports. The city wasn't that close and nobody had any money to travel, let alone to spend on fast food or clothes once we got there. I don't think I ever spent any waking hour at Monolit more than ten feet away from a ball.

There was no room for transgressions, and anyone caught breaking the rules was sent home. No one smoked. None of the older kids drank alcohol. Every night before curfew at ten o'clock, the coaches went through all the rooms and made sure the lights were off. A few kids with wealthier parents had TVs in their rooms, but by ten the screens went dark too.

I realised at some point that I was sacrificing quite a lot for the vague promise of becoming one of the 0.01 per cent of players who really make it. My friends were at home having fun, meeting girls, doing all sorts of cool things while I was basically getting up with the birds for work six days a week. On many occasions, I was envious of them and their normal lives. But then I always asked myself the all-important question: what did I want more? To hang out and drink beer or play football? The answer was obvious, as was the conclusion. I had to be fully committed to my goal, because otherwise I would be certain to lose out either way. There were no shortcuts to where I was trying to go.

You were forced to dedicate your life to football at Monolit. School was still important, but I'm not proud to say my grades suffered a little the longer I was there. I went down to a seven on average, which was still okay but not amazing.

As much as I loved every minute of being there, I did cry into my pillow at night for the first couple of weeks or so because I missed home dearly. You had to grow up very quickly and learn to control your emotions as a scholar. The coaches were a big help in that respect. They became family. In my case, literally so. Not long after I signed with the academy, my parents divorced. They had grown apart because of all of my dad's travelling. Now that I was no longer around, they felt they could both move on.

Viktor was also a recent divorcee. One of those days when parents came in to see their children, on weekends or public holidays, he and my mum started talking over food. One thing led to another and he became my stepdad. Having a stepdad who's also a football coach is potentially a complex dynamic. The roles can get blurred. But it was never a problem for us. Viktor was like an older friend to me, a mentor. He never tried to replace my father. And he was an incredibly hard worker, the hardest worker I have ever seen. When I spent time at home with him and Mum, we often drove to the countryside and went on long runs in the morning at six. We played backgammon and Uno, and the games were always super competitive. Tennis: hours and hours. At first I had no chance, then I started beating him. My life was even more dominated by sports after he and Mum got together. But he never pressurised me to do anything. He didn't have to. Having him was a blessing for me.

But then there was another disruption, and I had to move yet again. Monolit was shutting down. The academy, we were told, was in financial trouble and had to stop coaching kids in a few months. Everyone would get released. To say it was a shock for everybody doesn't do justice to the pain we all felt. Just when our dreams had begun to take shape, it was all over again. We'd be out on the street.

There was a big scramble to find academy places elsewhere. Monolit were the third-best youth development centre behind Shakhtar and Dynamo Kyiv, and there were rumours the most promising candidates might get a trial there. But the vast majority of us weren't quite good enough to make the cut at the big two, which meant the only way was down. The boys were distraught. Through no fault of their own, their chances of turning pro had taken a massive hit.

2

The Big Freeze

The German doctor looked at me gravely. 'You are fortunate,' he said. 'You came at the right time. Any later, and you might have lost your leg.'

I was 17 years old, stuck miles away from my home and family in a hospital near Hoffenheim in Germany. Luckily, one of the nurses was Ukrainian. She looked after me, spoke my language and spelled out what had happened. She told me: 'You're a lucky boy. The doctor thought about cutting your foot off.' Only then did I realise quite how close my dreams had come to ending and my life changing utterly.

I had gone there to try out for one of the best sides in Europe for a young player: TSG Hoffenheim. Roberto Firmino was playing for them, Demba Ba had been there. Their reputation was for taking unknown players and giving them a platform for big international moves. I was a teenager with few prospects, without a club, trying to make my way in Russia playing in street leagues. I had travelled to Germany to change my life forever. It almost did, just not in the way I expected. I never even got to do my trial for Hoffenheim. Rather, I almost ended my career forever in a German hospital with my foot amputated.

It's a long story to explain the journey of how I ended up there discussing the surgical removal of my foot. Looking back, there were moments along the way where I felt lost, but this one was certainly the most traumatic. When you rewrite the story, knowing the conclusion – playing for Manchester City, winning the Premier League, FA Cup and Carabao Cup, earning a great move to Arsenal – it's easier to contextualise those awful moments and tell yourself you were on some kind of inevitable route to this great destination. But when you're a teenager, it can feel like the world has ended, like you're never going to make it, that no one will ever notice you. My path was far from easy.

Leaving home, leaving my country, leaving my family, making myself vulnerable in a world of big business, smart agents and clever football executives... It turned out well, but there were several points on the way where I could have taken a different path and ended in a much worse place. Monolit closing down forced me to find a new place to continue my education as a footballer. Viktor felt I was good enough to get a trial at either Shakhtar Donetsk or Dynamo Kyiv. Just the thought of those teams got me hugely excited. They are like Real Madrid or Barcelona to Ukrainians. Those two dominate our football world and the dream of every Ukrainian kid is to play for one of them. In fact, when I was eight years old, I was playing in a game and my coach told me at the end that a scout from Shakhtar Donetsk had been watching me. On that occasion it was just talk. Nothing happened.

Viktor said I could choose either club, but his advice was to go to Shakhtar because the academy there was amazing due to the money that billionaire businessman Rinat Akhmetov had put into the club. Apparently, their facilities and the level of coaching were the best. On top of that, I had been a Shakhtar fan since childhood. They were my club. But part of me was very nervous. Shakhtar always had the best boys from all over the country in every age group. As a club, they set the benchmark in terms of quality. You worry whether you can fit in there, whether it will be your level.

So, with two boys from other teams, I went for a trial. And the standard was so high! I immediately felt like I had jumped a level. Afterwards, I suspected that I hadn't done nearly enough to stay. The two other guys I came with seemed to have played so much better than me. In fact, when I talk to friends who were at that trial – because many who were in that youth team play for the national team today – even now, they tell me the other guys had been much more impressive! But in the end, guess what? I stayed. And the other two guys went home. Ciao, ciao!

And so I moved again, to Donetsk in the east of Ukraine. My mum and Viktor rented a place in the Black Sea city of Mariupol, where he got a new job and managed to find a club for six of his former Monolit pupils. Mariupol was only 100 kilometres to the south, which made it easier to see them whenever I came home for a few days from Donetsk. And I had a few friends I knew from Monolit to hang out with there, too.

I was by now quite used to living away from my family. I had already made that break with home, I had become more mature, and I was so happy when I arrived in Donetsk. It wasn't just the quality of football that was at a higher level, the facilities were also a dream, like my coach at Monolit had promised. Pitch after pitch to train on, all of them perfect as if the groundsman had tended to them with his nail scissors. The food was incredibly good and nutritious. The kit was smart and there was so much of it: tracksuits, training tops, everything. There was a swimming pool too. For a 13-year-old, it all felt as if you were taken really seriously as a prospect and were close to being a pro. I didn't appreciate then that there were still a million things that could throw a spanner in the works.

Of course, it's still hard being away from your parents and friends. And back then we couldn't afford to use the internet much. No smartphones for us, just a SIM card and a brick phone to call home. That wasn't a bad thing, however. It forced us to make friends and start inventing our own games, mucking around and running about in our spare time. These days a kid can be glued to a device from the age of seven. We didn't have that.

I was interested only in football anyway. Oleksandr Funderat, Shakhtar's academy director, had a rule that everyone needed to rest in the evenings and recover, but

I kept sneaking out to football fields off-campus so that I wouldn't be seen practising more. He found out, however, and called me into his office. The fee for breaking rules was $20, and the director said that if I got caught again, I would have to pay. Shakhtar paid me about $100 in scholarship per month. But I told the director very earnestly that he could keep all the money and let me continue to play in the evenings instead. He laughed and talked me out of it in the end.

I was so serious about football that the other kids called me 'did' – grandfather in Ukrainian. They said I hardly smiled and was always frowning. But I hadn't come to mess around. I wanted to make it as a footballer.

My team was the class born in 1996 and we were probably the best generation Ukraine had had in a long time. We won four successive academy league titles while I was there. No one had done that before, and no one has done it since. Of my group, ten of us went on to play in the Under-19 national team. That's an incredible success rate, considering that so many youngsters don't make it. The boys at Shakhtar were essentially the future national team of Ukraine. At times I felt like I wasn't even close, in terms of talent, to some of those guys. And yet I don't even know where some of them are today or whether they're still playing.

At 15, I was selected for the junior national side, but I was one of the smaller kids, having been born in December, and couldn't get into the team. Then Viktor Kovalenko got injured during the Under-17 Euro qualifiers against

Estonia and I was suddenly in for 26 minutes. I also played ten minutes against Bulgaria. Ahead of the next game, against Germany – a side that included Jonathan Tah, Julian Brandt and Timo Werner – the coach pulled me aside for little talk. 'Everything is good,' he told me, 'but you're playing too fast. Slow down a little.'

I asked Viktor what I should do. He said, 'If you want to be like everyone else, then play like everyone else. But if you want to be an exceptional player, then continue playing fast like you have been.' I had a good game. We beat the Germans 1-0 and qualified for the tournament in Slovakia.

I was really enjoying myself. We had a great team. I was 16 but one of the captains of the Under-19s and playing in the Youth Champions League, a new competition for academy teams of clubs that were in the Champions League. It was an amazing experience. We played in Spain against Real Sociedad and in Germany against Bayer Leverkusen. But of course the game we all looked forward to was against Manchester United, who were also in our group. Their team came to Donetsk and I remember Andreas Pereira played and Dean Henderson was on the bench. We took the lead when Liam Grimshaw deflected in my free kick, but they equalised in the second half before Alex Zubkov, now my team-mate on the national team, scored the winner on 87 minutes. It was an incredible performance and the coaches were really pleased with us. We were showing the world what Shakhtar could do.

We then went to Manchester to play them and I scored on 76 minutes. They got a late equaliser, but we finished second in the group behind Real Sociedad and above United. The club were really pleased we were showing ourselves so well on the international stage and leaving giants like United in our wake. My life was on a perfect trajectory. This was how I imagined it.

And then came my first experience of football politics. I couldn't have dreamed how it was going to affect me, how desperate I would become, how little agency I had in a struggle over a contract. And how it would ultimately lead me to that hospital in Germany.

I only ever had one question for Shakhtar. I was loving my life, we were playing well as a team, impressing people all over Europe. I was an occasional captain. All I asked was, 'Do you genuinely see me as someone who can play in the first team? Or am I just Shakhtar player No. 305, who will be sent out on loan to a different club every season?'

Shakhtar had all these amazing Brazilians playing for them: Willian, Fernandinho, Douglas Costa and Alex Teixeira. Henrikh Mkhitaryan, the Armenian midfielder who would later play for Borussia Dortmund, Manchester United and Arsenal, was also there. Making the first team was really tough for Ukrainian players during that spell, if not impossible. There was always some Brazilian kid they could sign, develop and sell on for huge fees instead. You could end up knocking on the door forever and never getting in. I was 16, and the next few years were so important for me to make the transition to adult football.

To be fair, they were straight with me and Anatoliy Patuk, an acquaintance of Viktor's who had started to act as an advisor to me. 'To be honest, we see you more in the category of a loan player than a first team,' they said.

We had just qualified for the knockout stages of the Youth Champions League and were playing Arsenal in the next round, another glamour tie. The winter break was coming. I was about to turn 17. I said: 'Look, if that's how you feel, let's wait until after the Youth Champions League game and speak then. I really want to be a first-team player here. I don't want an answer straight away, I am patient. But I need to know that breaking into the first team is a realistic goal. Let's wait and see. I'm sure we'll reach a solution, but I don't want to sign an extension just yet. I still have almost two years.' The money they were offering was not great either, in all honesty. But it wasn't even about that. I just had to know there was a pathway to the first team before I committed.

I was third captain of the team, so I guess they were worried I might leave one day, though I still had almost two years left on my contract. But I was quite naive, just enjoying my football and the fact we were getting noticed throughout Europe. Clubs are always scared you might run down your contract, and then the statutory compensation fee they receive is much lower than a transfer fee. By extending my contract, they were protecting my value, which made total sense from their point of view.

THE BIG FREEZE

But I didn't want to be rushed into committing to anything. I wanted to understand what kind of future I had at Shakhtar.

But they didn't want to wait. 'No, you need to sign now!' club officials were saying. 'If you're not going to extend your contract with us, then you're not going to play for the Under-19 team at all! You'll miss the Arsenal game. And you can't train with us if you don't extend. It will mean no more football for you.'

Because of the way football works, you can't just join another club if your club freezes you out. I still was under contract, and FIFA rules say the club that owns you has to agree to let you train or join another club, normally after compensation has been paid. Most players in my situation cave in and sign an extension. You need to play, especially when you're so young. It was hard to know what to do. I wasn't sure that it was best to extend the contract. So I held my ground.

That's how I came to be running laps of the training ground while my team-mates prepared for the Arsenal game. For four months I didn't play at all. It was the winter break in Ukraine, and there weren't any national team games either. When we came back after the break in February 2014, I was left to my own devices, banished. They wouldn't let me join in any team training and sent me to run those laps instead. They made good on their promise that they would freeze me out. Imagine that. I had just turned 17; I was a kid who wanted to play. But they were looking at this from a business angle, and I understood pretty quickly this wasn't personal. Losing me for next to nothing after investing so much time and money would have been a disaster for them. So the gloves were off.

There was a lot of pressure on me to do what the club wanted, but the people around me, my family and Anatoliy, stayed calm, supporting my stance. But every day I was watching my team-mates having fun, working hard, playing, training and preparing for this massive game against Arsenal. I was alone, isolated, running laps, and thought I was being punished for not doing what the club wanted. I believe they made an example of me, sending a message to the others: 'This is what happens to a player who doesn't sign his contract extension.' The bosses kept saying: 'Just sign this piece of paper. Everything will be all right.'

The away game against Arsenal was coming up and I was desperate to get back onto the pitch. Arsenal were the English team I supported as a boy. But I had hardly trained with the team. I was still doing most of the exercises on my own. On the day of the match, they put the contract on my table and asked me once more. I didn't sign it and prepared myself for watching the game from the stand. Then, at the last minute, they decided to play me anyway. It was crazy, because I hadn't trained properly at all. But I guess they wanted to show off their best players on their trip to England.

This Arsenal side had Serge Gnabry, Héctor Bellerín and Chuba Akpom. I played at No. 10 for that game. We went 1-0 down, but just before half-time I took a free kick that fell to Andriy Boryachuk, who is now a pro with

Metalist Kharkiv, and he equalised. We lost 3-1. For reasons I will go into later, it still proved a memorable and pivotal occasion. It would change my life.

But not at that point.

Right then, the game didn't change anything. I was still in limbo at Shakhtar. I trained alone. And what made it harder to accept was that I had a great coach there in Valeriy Kryventsov. In fact, the time I spent in Shakhtar playing for him was one of the best times of my life, the contractual dispute aside.

But some things were tough to swallow. Ukraine had a big chance to play in the Under-20 World Cup, which was due to be staged the following year, in May 2015. I was certain to go. But the manager told me straight up: 'You won't be there next year unless you extend with Shakhtar.' It wasn't so much a threat as a prediction, and entirely accurate. I stopped getting called up by youth teams altogether and didn't go to the World Cup either. It was painful, not being in control of your own career like that.

During those four months when I wasn't playing, I kept busy in different ways. I used to bug the team analyst, the guy who had all the video clips of my games. I got him to make a compilation of my best moments and put them on a memory card. In the end I had this eight-minute showreel with all my highlights from games, including the Youth Champions League matches. We must have sent this USB stick to every club we could think of, including all the sides in the Russian division. Still, no one wanted to know. They would write back and say: 'No thanks. We have plenty of talent in our academies.'

In the meantime, Ukraine had plunged into crisis. The first stage of the war had arrived in February 2014 when Russia occupied Crimea illegally, with very little resistance. And in April they started trouble in the Donbas region, as Russian-backed militias began to seize towns. Our stadium was damaged by bombs, and the first team had to play their home games in Lviv, 1,200 kilometres away at the other end of the country. Meanwhile, they were giving out Russian passports to everybody and proclaimed Donetsk a Russian city. I didn't understand what was happening. Up until that moment, I had paid very little attention to politics. I was still very fixed on my football career. That was everything to me. All I was worried about was that I had to leave Shakhtar because they wouldn't let me play.

I know some people question why I would choose to go to Russia of all places at that time. Believe me, it is not something I would ever do again. But I had no other options. I had no club or opportunity elsewhere in Europe. In fact, I hardly even had options inside Russia. But my agent had some connections there and we felt it was my best chance. Why couldn't I just try another Ukrainian club? Shakhtar were too powerful for that. If I had approached another club, they would have just blocked it. No club could stand up to them. It was impossible. I was like a bird in a cage in Ukraine, trapped with no way out. I had to leave the country.

Despite this rather sad ending to my time with Shakhtar, I will always love the club dearly. My feelings for them have never changed. I can see myself going back there again one day, perhaps as a manager. Some of the people I dealt with then are still there today, and we have a great relationship. They can understand my reasons and I can understand theirs. Football is also a business. Sometimes, conflict is unavoidable.

Russia wasn't even a particularly promising option, but it was at least a possibility. I've always wanted to explain this properly to Ukraine fans, because they have been the best in the world in supporting the team and country. It just seemed like the only football option I had, and I was too young and uninformed to understand the situation properly. My eyes opened only a couple of years later.

I went to Moscow in the summer of 2014 with my agent because we thought there would be more opportunities there. I didn't have any offers. No one was waiting for me. My USB video clips didn't have scouts or agents ringing. Nothing. I was surviving off Anatoliy's money, living in a garage apartment next to his home. It was a simple set-up, but I was grateful for his help. I didn't complain. I wasn't born to luxury; I'm from a small city. I'm a big believer in the mantra that adversity makes you stronger. You learn to adapt to any situation and look at the positives, especially when you're hungry to get ahead.

When you come from little, you have nothing to lose. You just go for it and you take it. If you're too comfortable as a young player, you might not have the same motivation, and then you won't make it. Anatoliy had some good Russian contacts who tried to fix me up with a club, but they were getting the same responses from Zenit and Spartak Moscow. Their academies were full. They wanted Brazilians. Certainly not some skinny Ukrainian kid.

I still couldn't play for another club, because my contract with Shakhtar ran for another year. Nobody wanted even to give me the chance to show what I could do in a trial, so I briefly thought about giving up. This was the darkest hour. I felt invisible. No one wanted to see me. I couldn't even get judged on whether I was good enough or not. But I had enough trust in myself to carry on and worked even harder. Deep down, I was sure my chances would come. I had played in the Ukraine youth teams, in the Youth Champions League with Shakhtar. Surely, someone somewhere would give me a shot?

To keep fit and make a bit of money on the side, I played in street teams and amateur tournaments, nine-a-side games, some 11-a-side games but on clay, concrete, grass, whatever. If they needed a player, I was there. Some guys I was up against were twice my age and real bruisers with experience in the Russian second division. Referees didn't care about fouls. It was a brutal education after playing academy football for so many years. But that didn't faze me. I needed the games. And for a 17-year-old unemployed footballer, getting the equivalent of $100 a week was good money. That said, we only got paid if we won. It was strictly: 'No win, no fee!'

THE BIG FREEZE

Finally, a call did come. And not just from anywhere. From Germany, a Bundesliga side: TSG Hoffenheim. This is when my story could have turned tragic. But it is still a strange tale as to how I got from the excitement of travelling to a Bundesliga team to almost having my foot amputated.

After all the waiting, I was so excited to be going to Germany. I believed all my problems would be over if I could convince them to take me on. There was a clear path, not just to their first team, but maybe beyond. But the day before I was due to fly there, FC Meteor, one of the non-league clubs I played for, called me. They had a big game and wanted me to fill in. They had been good to me, so I didn't want to let them down. And what harm could another game do?

I mentioned these leagues were a bit rogue, sometimes more like a cage fight. Of course, this was the day some opponent did a crazy tackle on me and caught my right ankle. It swelled up like a balloon. There was no way I could play the next day in Germany. Just walking was causing me pain. I was in no state to do a trial. But I couldn't cancel and lose this life-changing opportunity. We decided I would go anyway and ask them to let me train a couple of days later, by which time the swelling would have hopefully gone down.

And here's how I almost lost my foot, career and professional life. I was on the plane with Lufthansa and I remember thinking, 'Let's not waste time to get the swelling down. Let's use the flight.' So I asked the stewardess for some ice for my ankle. She didn't understand me at first because my English wasn't great and I didn't speak any German. But she came over with what looked like ice in a plastic package. I wrapped it up, put it on my ankle and went to sleep. Problem solved.

An hour or so later, I woke up and expected to see a bag full of melted water. But there was none, just an empty plastic package. I didn't understand. Then I looked at my ankle. All the skin had turned white. I put my sock back on and, within around 20 minutes, as it warmed up, it started to blister. There were massive blisters all over my ankle where the ice had been. By now I was worried. This didn't seem right. How could my ankle be reacting like this?

When we arrived in Frankfurt, an associate of my agent was waiting. 'I have a little problem,' I told him. I think I gave him the shock of his life when I showed him my ankle. He nearly keeled over. 'What the hell is this?!' he stammered. 'I've never seen this before.'

We drove to the Hoffenheim academy, as my trial was for their Under-21s and they had a medical team there. The guy who accompanied me was worried, but I still hadn't appreciated the full seriousness of the situation. We were taken immediately to a physio, who pulled down my sock and turned nearly as white as the skin on my ankle when he saw it. His reaction told me this was bad. 'We're taking you to hospital, right now,' he said. Again, when I arrived at the hospital, every nurse and doctor had the same reaction. I was rushed into an operating theatre and surgery commenced immediately. They were removing gangrenous tissue. If that had spread, it could have affected the whole foot, requiring it all to be removed.

The reason? I had frostbite. It turned out that when the air stewardess gave me ice, it was dry ice, which is three times colder than normal ice. And it doesn't melt into water, but converts to its gaseous form as it warms. It had been like exposing my bare ankle to Arctic-like temperatures. The blood to my ankle had been completely cut off and the vessels were so badly damaged that the tissue was dead. Had we not got to the hospital quickly, the gangrene could have spread and then, to save your life, they have to amputate the affected area. Like the Ukrainian nurse said, I was a lucky boy. Very lucky.

It was a horrible experience. I was all by myself in a foreign country and had just found out my career could very nearly have been over before it had even started properly. I still didn't know for sure how I would recover. I was praying that I would at least be able just to walk and jog again. I had two weeks in that hospital before they would let me go home. By then, although some of my muscles had wasted, I was recovering. It looked like I would play again. And nowadays, apart from a huge scar that still frightens team-mates and physios when they see it, everything is normal.

3

Catching a Break

Nearly losing my foot in Germany put my predicament into perspective. But when I returned to Moscow, I was back to my old life, hustling for games. Nothing had changed. I was still miles away from a professional football career. My hopes receded, but just when it seemed all was lost, a call came. Rubin Kazan, a team about 750 kilometres east of Moscow, rang Anatoliy. That USB stick had finally come good! They remembered my video clips, liked what they had seen and asked whether I would like to go for pre-season training. They understood the situation with Shakhtar, that I was not a fully free agent yet and that there would be some issues getting the transfer through UEFA and FIFA. But they were a Russian club, and therefore less worried about Shakhtar. After so many months without a club and being unable to play, it felt amazing.

It was potentially a great opportunity. Marko Dević, the Serb who had a Ukraine passport and played for the national team, was there. We went to Italy to train pre-season and I did well. Coach Rinat Bilyaletdinov said I made a magnificent impression and he really wanted me. The club, too, said they wanted me. They were telling me every week: 'Alex, next week we're going to give you a contract.'

So I stayed there for four months waiting, waiting, living in a room at the training ground and playing only friendly games, because I couldn't register for the first team until they had sorted things out with Shakhtar. I trained every day with the team, but I needed to play. And I had no money. I lived off an allowance from my agent. The promised contract never arrived. Agreeing a deal with Shakhtar was apparently too complicated. It was an untenable situation. I had to take a decision.

One day, I just packed my bags and got a flight back to Moscow. It was hard to walk away from Kazan, but it was obvious they couldn't get me out of my predicament. I found myself in my agent's garage in Moscow again. Back to square one. Like a game of snakes and ladders, I kept finding myself back at the beginning of my journey, miles from getting a proper club.

But in early 2015, my agent had one last option. FC Ufa were keen. They were a new team in Russia, founded in 2010. But they had backing from the president of the Republic of Bashkortostan, part of the Russian Federation, and they were now in the Premier League. It was even further away than Kazan, though. Ufa is about

1,000 kilometres east of Moscow. But once I had another small procedure on my ankle, they were willing to take me. I was to join them for the mid-season training camp, before the season restarted in the spring. They agreed to give me a contract and said they would take on Shakhtar over the legal issues, as I was still contracted to them for four more months.

They took a chance on me, and I'll always be grateful for that. It was a huge relief just to be part of a proper team again after being in limbo for so long. I was so happy. There was still legal wrangling going on with Shakhtar, and they claimed I couldn't play for FC Ufa. But FIFA ruled I could sign a provisional contract and play from March onwards. Shakhtar received €5,000 from Ufa by way of compensation. The club set up me and my mum in an apartment in Ufa. After everything we had been through, it felt like a normal life again.

It was amazing to be playing senior football at this level, but I had a lot of work to do to convince the locals and the team. No one had ever heard of me. They invited the press for a big presentation, teasing that they were announcing this great new signing. You can imagine how disappointed everyone was to see an unknown Ukrainian kid. It wasn't what the fans and press had in mind for a grand unveiling. But for me it was a new start and I was determined to seize my chance.

When I made my debut, coming on against FK Krasnodar in March 2015, it was more than a year since that Youth Champions League game with Arsenal, my last match for Shakhtar. Though we lost 2-0, I did well when I came on at half-time. I created two big chances for my team-mates and everyone started to talk about me. That was a real confidence boost. It felt like I was back in the swing of things again. And within a few games, I was starting for the first team.

I had to become a man overnight, going from youth football to the big boys. I was playing against veterans, guys with years of knowledge who were physically stronger. Hulk, Axel Witsel and Branislav Ivanović played in this league. These were huge names, Champions League winners, Europa League winners, internationals with Brazil, Belgium and Serbia. This wasn't academy football any more. Every single point, every single game really mattered. And players were fighting for their next contract, for their livelihood. Some guys were really good to me. Emmanuel Frimpong was at the club and I persuaded him to teach me some English. He had been at Arsenal and, in my head, I was already preparing for a day when I wouldn't be in Russia or Ukraine. He gave me a few lessons, which really helped.

Slowly I earned the respect of press and players. The Ukrainian FA, who hadn't called me up to any youth internationals since I stopped playing for Shakhtar, remembered me too. I played for the Under-19s in the Euro qualifiers and the three group games at the tournament in Greece. We were knocked out with one point from nine, but there was a bit of hype building. People were talking about me so much that there were rumours in the press that I might become Russian. It was an easy process for Ukrainians to get Russian citizenship, in just a matter of weeks. I think the club would have liked that, as I wouldn't be counted as a foreign player. The press were saying it would be a smart move for Russia. Social media was full of speculation. Some famous ex-Russia players were saying, 'We need to give him a passport. Now.' I guess the Ukrainian Federation became a bit scared about this talk.

But it was never a consideration. Never, ever. Even before the invasion in 2022, becoming a player for the Russian national team was an impossibility for me. I am Ukrainian and I love my country.

After one game with the Under-21s, a 1-0 home defeat by Iceland, our manager, Sergiy Kovalets, called me into his office and said: 'Alex, tomorrow you are travelling to join the first team, the national team. They have a game against Spain, qualification for Euro 2016. A car will pick you up in the morning. The manager, Mykhaylo Fomenko, wants you in the squad.' I was in Cherkasy with the Under-21s, about 200 kilometres south of Kyiv, so I had to get the car the next morning to join the senior squad.

I was surprised, but I could also see what the Ukrainian Football Federation were up to. FIFA rules said you could switch nations at any time if you had played for the Under-21s or younger age-group teams, and even if you had played a friendly game for the senior national team. But as soon as you played for your senior national team in an official Euro or World Cup game, even a qualifier, that was it. That was your football country for life. They had obviously decided to bring me on in this official Euro 2016 qualifier against Spain for a couple of minutes to ensure I could never play for Russia. Of course, there was no chance of that ever happening from my point of view, anyway. But I went along with this ploy. Getting my first cap was still a huge honour. It would help stop the silly rumours and settle the issue once and for all. I was only ever playing for Ukraine.

When I got to the hotel to join the national team, I was so scared! There were all these legends walking around me, players I had grown up watching. Now there is a new generation, but back then there were quite a few old, experienced players. Who are we talking about? Oleg Gusev, the Dynamo Kyiv player, as well as Shakhtar legends Vyacheslav Shevchuk, Alex Kucher, Artem Fedetskyi and Yaroslav Rakitskyi. There was Andriy Yarmolenko, who would go on to play for Borussia Dortmund and West Ham, and Yevhen Konoplyanka, a Europa League winner at Sevilla that season. I was so much in awe of them that I just went straight to my room and was too timid to come out.

The national team set-up was still very traditional then, very hierarchical. The older guys called the shots; they were untouchable. As a young player, you had to do as you were told and be quiet. It was the same in all the professional teams I had played in.

Later, when I moved to City, I realised it didn't have to be this way, however. Football is a team sport. You are

CATCHING A BREAK

one family. You can all push each other. Why should it matter how old you are? Ruben Diaz was younger than me, but he explained what I had to do to help him in City's backline. He didn't put himself above me, he didn't lecture me. What needed to be said was said. And that went the other way, too. There were plenty of times when I told him things I thought would benefit him and the team. If you're just playing your own game, not paying attention to others and making no effort to support them with some shouts during the game, it's hard for the players around you to improve. As a result, you won't improve either.

I remember a young player told me he found it hard to speak to the more established pros on the pitch. 'I don't know how they will react,' he said to me. I replied: 'It's not about young players, old players, or experience. We are all in the same position. Think of a sauna. We are all naked there. We are all there to get hot and sweaty. There's no difference. It's the same thing on the pitch, aside from wearing clothes, of course. We are all doing the same job. And we all play better when our team-mates are looking out for us.'

And I did come on for a few minutes against Spain – the reigning Euro champions from 2012 – replacing Rotan on 87 minutes. Spain had Cesc Fabregas, Cesar Azpilicueta, Thiago, Sergio Busquets, Juan Mata and Isco. The game was at the Olympic Stadium in Kyiv, with a capacity crowd, but I doubt anybody knew me. They must have wondered why the coach brought me on at 1-0 down with three minutes to go. 'Who is this guy?' everyone thought. I actually had an opportunity to equalise. I received the ball at the edge of the box. Nacho challenged me but I went to the right, got past him and shaped to shoot with my right foot. But Busquets just came alongside me and nicked the ball. With all his experience, he had read my intentions perfectly, probably before I even had that thought myself! It could have been a glorious start to my national team career. But that's what happens when you're up against the best players in the world.

I had made my debut, at least. Now I was Ukraine forever. And so proud.

I continued to do well for FC Ufa. Scouts from Marseille showed up at one of our games and talked to me briefly. Then my agent received a call from Germany: Borussia Dortmund wanted to see me. Thomas Tuchel was the coach. It was the first season after Jürgen Klopp's departure. Of course we jumped straight onto the next available plane. The invitation was timed for a BVB home game in the Europa League. While we were watching the match, someone from the scouting department came to greet us.

He said, 'Nice to meet you. Look, keep working hard. We have our eyes on you.' And then he left. That was it. My agent and I looked at each other. Did we really just come all the way for a handshake and some warm words? Unfortunately, yes. They weren't really interested. Not yet, in any case. I could understand them, in all honesty. I hadn't done enough to go to Dortmund yet.

My form was picking up, however. I played really well, scored at Zenit in December 2015 and we almost won, if it hadn't been for a late equaliser. There was a lot of talk in the press after that game. Russian papers were suggesting that Zenit were considering me as an option for the following season. Zenit were the club that picked up all the best players in the Russian Premier League. And people in Ukraine started to say I had a chance for Euro 2016 in France.

That seemed fanciful, since I hadn't been picked for the senior team again after playing those few minutes against Spain. They won the play-off against Slovenia in November to qualify for the Euros, winning 3-1 on aggregate without me. I began to dream. Maybe there was a chance I could sneak into the squad? But again, there were non-football factors at play that impeded my chances to succeed in the background. Things got very political.

I was invited to join the Under-21 team in March. I arrived at the training camp, got changed, stepped onto the grass, ready to start. Then my manager, Oleksandr Holovko, came over. He said to me: 'Alex, because of the situation between our countries, the decision has been made by the people above that players based in Russia will not play for Ukraine. You need to go to the dressing room, go to your club and sort things out with them.' I was in shock. I hadn't even touched a ball and was already on a flight back to Ufa.

That came as a huge shock to me. Firstly, I had only just got myself sorted again. Secondly, as I said before, I had been so single-minded in my career. I had stopped looking at what was going on around me. I hadn't appreciated how bad the situation had become between the countries. Now, I can understand why they spoke to me like that. Then, I was just thrown into more confusion and worry.

Moving clubs was impossible in the middle of the season. And I had only just begun to play regular football at the highest level again. But that conversation with Holovko also had an incentive, something that had blown me away and filled me with hope. 'I know you're in the first team manager's thoughts for the Euros,' he said. Ukraine were close to qualifying for Euro 2016 in France.

Was Holovko serious or just being nice to me? If I really had a small chance, I swore to myself I would take it. At the very least, I set myself a target of making it to the provisional list of 30 players. Then the manager could whittle them down to the best 23. I just had to continue to play well for Ufa.

While all these rumours about me changing clubs were swirling around, we were fighting a relegation battle. And I was beginning to get attention of the unwanted kind. Opposition players started to target me. When we played against Rubin Kazan at home, a guy went for me and stamped on my left foot a few minutes into the game. Usually, when someone steps on your foot or you get a kick, you have so much adrenaline that you don't feel it. You forget about it until later. But as soon as I put weight on my left foot again that day, I was in agony. I somehow continued for the rest of the first half. During the break, I had my little toe checked. 'Looks like you didn't break it,' the doctor said. He put a few injections in it to numb the pain. In the second half, I didn't feel anything. We finished the game 1-1.

The next day, my toe had swollen up so much that it was bigger than my big toe. It didn't take an expert to see it was broken – you could have seen that a mile off. I took myself to the hospital. They did a scan and my suspicion was right: the main bone was broken. They put me in a plaster that went all the way up to my knee! I was like, 'Really? I only broke my toe!' This was early May, two weeks before the Euro 2016 squad would be announced. We also had a big relegation fight on our hands, and I was hobbling around in plaster and on crutches, all because of a broken toe? The doctor at the hospital said: 'Don't move for three to four weeks. Don't put any pressure on it. Take it easy!' Three weeks? My Euro dreams were over. And I could no longer help the team avoid the drop, either.

I couldn't accept that. At home, I took off the cast straight away and told the club doctor, 'If there's even a small chance I can make it to the Euros, I will try.' But they wanted me to play straight away. The next FC Ufa game was Amkar away, a direct rival of ours in the relegation battle. A classic six-pointer. I didn't train for three days. Of course the club really wanted me to play, broken toe or not. And these guys had given me the chance to become a professional, so I felt I owed them. The day before the match, they gave me an injection, but even so, I felt so much pain. The hardest thing was to wear boots. There was so much pain as soon as they touched my toe. I walked around in flip-flops during the day because it was just too painful otherwise. As soon as I put boots on, with their tight fit, it was excruciating. In the end, I played the full 90 minutes but we lost 1-0, Amkar scoring from a free kick.

One FC Ufa director was furious with everyone and came down to the dressing room. And in front of everyone, he singled me out and said: 'You're not going anywhere. You're going to stay with us, even if we go down to the second division.' There was all this talk about a transfer for me, so he was fuming. But it was crazy. It wasn't my fault we had lost. I had literally played with a broken toe to help the team!

For the last game, we played Spartak Moscow at home. It was now a massive match that would decide whether we stayed in the Russian Premier League or not. Spartak is a big club. They were fighting for the title, we were fighting against relegation. And even if we won, we still needed other results to go our way. But even the directors at FC Ufa had realised I was in no shape to play. Luckily, we won 3-1 without me, and the other results worked out for us. We survived and could celebrate. I had done my bit, even if that angry director didn't see it that way. Who knows what he would have said had we been relegated?

I still wasn't sure where I stood with the national team coach, however. The Euro 2016 squad was due to be announced five days after the season finished. I thought I could maybe make that longlist of 30 names and then at least have a chance to prove my fitness in training. That said, I did have a badly broken toe. But I was encouraged when Fomenko, the coach, called to check up on me. 'I read you had an injury issue and that's why you didn't play the last game. Is everything okay with you? Can you join us?' I was elated. 'Of course, all fine,' I said. 'Just a minor issue, nothing to worry about.' What else do you say? It's the Euros. I was in the provisional squad. I was never going to say: 'Well, my toe may be an issue …'.

I didn't do anything that week and continued to walk around in flip-flops. My broken toe was still hurting like hell. Even as I was packing to go for the squad meet-up, my agent was saying to me: 'What are you doing packing all this stuff?' I had packed everything, just in case I made the 23 and was there for six weeks. 'It's a waste of time; they're going to send you home as soon as they see the scan on your toe!' he said. But I had worked out this plan for arriving at the team camp. I would wear a trainer on the right foot and one flip-flop on my left travelling there. I would keep the spare trainer in my rucksack. As soon as I got to the hotel, I'd get the spare trainer out, quickly put it on, and no one would know there was a problem.

I went to the hotel, and we had a training session right away. And before the training, the doctor said to me, 'Okay, show me your scan. I heard you have some toe issue.' And I showed him the X-ray from the hospital. I'm not a doctor, but even I could see it wasn't right. The bone wasn't straight! He asked me how I felt. I replied, 'Yes, all okay. Ready to go!' And he said: 'Can you train?' 'Sure. I'm fine.' I was a young player on the fringes, so perhaps they didn't pay that much attention to me, but they didn't bother to conduct any more tests. They just went with what

I told them, trusting in my not-so-accurate self-diagnosis. I stayed and trained every day.

To this day, I have no idea how I did that because I was in agony non-stop. But I guess I really wanted to be there, to make the Euros. I had so much desire, it was such a big dream. I was starting to get used to the pain in training. I was almost enjoying fighting through it. That was a very strange sensation. But there were some significant issues. Because of how many injections I needed, the skin was opening up and weeping. The doctor told me I needed to cover it and clean it, because your feet sweat when you train, which can cause infections if the sweat gets into the wound. So, as soon as we finished sessions, I had to go to my room to clean everything and bandage it again. I was so desperate to make the squad that I just blanked out the pain. My desire helped me survive.

We did a couple of sessions and had a friendly game against Romania. I came on for the second half and, a few minutes later, made Ukrainian history! I scored, a left-footed strike from outside the box to make it 2-1. We won 4-3 and I was now the youngest player to score for the Ukraine national team. All with a broken toe. I was so proud. But more importantly, I thought: 'Now I've proved myself, surely I will make the final 23?'

That's when my agent got in touch with some extraordinary news. Remember, six months before I had been playing in street leagues in Moscow. Nine months before I had almost lost my foot. Even now I was with FC Ufa, a place where big teams don't often scout. So what he told me sounded like a cruel joke: 'Alex, Manchester City have made an enquiry about you.' Manchester City?! They were Premier League champions in 2014. They had just hired Pep Guardiola for the next season, the greatest coach in world football. This was ridiculous.

'Zenit, Dortmund, I get,' I said. 'But Man City?! Now you've gone too far!'

He assured me their interest was sincere. Apparently, they had been tracking me since that Youth Champions League game at Arsenal. It was a life-changing event after all! They wondered why I had dropped off the radar but had noticed me pop up again at Ufa. My head was in a whirl. I was on the verge of the Euros and a move no one could imagine. As would be immediately evident.

The Ukraine coach Fomenko called me in for a chat, to repeat the warning Holovko had given me a few months earlier. It was unacceptable for me to play in Russia. 'Alex, do you realise that if you've decided to carry on playing in Russia, you won't play for the national team any more?' By now I understood they were serious.

I had made up my mind that I wanted to leave Ufa in any case, because the way the season ended had made me uneasy about the people there. I felt this was a good time to share the potential good news with Fomenko. I told him I had some options abroad, and perhaps you will understand why I was a little reticent to share my news. And why even I struggled to comprehend it.

Fomenko is a guy who's always deadly serious. He never smiles, never shows any emotions at all. You would never know from his face if the team were 3-0 up or 3-0 down. He asked: 'Where?' And I said: 'Well, my agent heard from Manchester City. I might go there.' This stern coach, who never smiles, just looked at me and burst out laughing. This guy from FC Ufa, 18 years old? Manchester City?! It was obviously some joke. I nearly laughed with him, as I couldn't quite believe it either. I hadn't told anyone, for fear of jinxing it, but also because I knew most people would have that same kind of dismissive reaction.

There was a lot going on in my life. At least one objective was achieved. I made the final 23 for the Euros, a wish come true. Eighteen months before, I hadn't even had a club, and now I was going to Euro 2016.

We travelled to France full of hope. We knew our first game against Germany, the World Cup winners, would be tough, but we had every confidence we could get results against Northern Ireland and Poland to qualify for the knockout stages. We were based in Paris. Six months earlier, terrorists had gone on a rampage in the city centre. Security was incredibly tight. For nearly one month, we didn't leave the hotel. I was already quite scared to leave my room and mix with the more established players, which made my experience even more claustrophobic. It was a crazy time. And yet, the thrill of being there outweighed all the anxiety.

The first game in Lille went okay, despite the 2-0 defeat. We conceded a lot of possession to Germany, as expected, but kept the game open. After going 1-0 down to a Shkodran Mustafi header, Jérôme Boateng made an unbelievable goal-line clearance to take Germany's narrow lead into the break. Bastian Schweinsteiger scored their second goal on the counter-attack, when we were throwing men forward with abandon to get the equaliser deep in injury time. And for me, the next dream had come true. On 73 minutes, I had come on for Viktor Kovalenko. I had played a game at the European Championship!

Representing my country at a big tournament was one of the best feelings in my life. Sharing the pitch with these players had been inconceivable not long ago, beyond anything I could have imagined. This was a big moment for me. It made me realise that everything is possible in life.

If I'm honest with myself, I didn't feel I had the right to be in the same team as these guys when it came to raw ability. When I looked back to that Shakhtar class of '96, probably the best generation Ukraine had seen, so many were incredible players, and I was not even close to them in terms of skills. But some of them couldn't stay the course. There are things you cannot control – injuries, for example – but the difference is mentality. If you're hungry enough, if you work hard enough, you can go all the way. And now here I was, playing at the Euros.

We felt confident going into the Northern Ireland game. We were above them in the FIFA rankings, though everyone knew this was a good side that had qualified for their first tournament for 30 years. Still, we expected and hoped to win. But this time the dynamic of the game was the complete opposite to the Germany one. We had all the possession and Northern Ireland were happy to let us have the ball. The trouble was we just couldn't create enough. And that classic thing happened when you're playing a side like that. They got a free kick on the edge of our area, worked their routine and scored, a header from Gareth McAuley. It came just after half-time. We had to try even harder just to get back in the game, but now they could sit even deeper and just defend.

Northern Ireland manager Michael O'Neill had done his homework perfectly. They were negating all our strengths. A hailstorm interrupted the match for a while. The referee stopped play, which was bizarre. But the weather matched our troubled state of mind. Nothing was going right. On 83 minutes, I came on but couldn't change anything. We conceded another late goal while pushing for an equaliser. Worse, Germany had drawn 0-0 with Poland, who had won their first game, which meant we were definitely out. We were devastated.

Everyone was very upset. Back home, the fans and the press were really disappointed in us. The third game, against Poland, was a dead rubber for us. In some ways, it was hard to motivate ourselves for it. But the team knew we had to show something. And I was definitely up for it. The manager was rotating and picked me to start my first game for the national team – in the No. 10 position.

It was Fomenko's last game in charge. He had already announced he would quit after losing the Northern Ireland game. But his last act was to show his faith in me, and I guess in the next generation of Ukrainian players, by backing a youngster. Him giving me such a key role got me noticed. The UEFA official match report said, 'Zinchenko was a bundle of energy and inventiveness in a free role behind Roman Zozulya, one through ball to the lone forward an indicator of his confidence on his maiden international start.' Nice one. Again, we dominated possession and created better chances this time. Ruslan Rotan was man of the match, so we hadn't played badly at all. But we lost once more, 1-0, to a Jakub Błaszczykowski goal. It was gutting.

I left France with very mixed emotions. As a team, we failed. Worse, we had been a disaster. We didn't get a point and didn't even score a single goal. Our pride was hurt. But for me personally, just being there was a huge boost for my career. Not long ago, I had lived in a garage and sent out USB sticks. Now I was staying with the national team at a UEFA VIP hotel and was getting name-checked at a major tournament. Most significantly of all, my agent was talking to Manchester City. Talking to, though. Nothing was agreed. It could still all go wrong. What if Ufa wouldn't let me go? What if City lost interest? What if it was all a big joke? I headed back to Moscow with all these questions in my head.

4

In But Out

City were one of the strongest sides in the Premier League, champions in 2014 and the club that had just appointed Pep Guardiola, by popular consensus the best manager in the world. And they were interested in me!

As soon as the Euros were over, with our 1-0 defeat to Poland, I flew from Paris to Ufa, but I had to change in Moscow, where I was to meet my agent. I had separate flights, rather than a continuous connecting flight to Ufa, so I had to check out and check in again, which gave us time to have a coffee, though my agent was telling me to get the ticket to Ufa first. But I looked at my watch and we had so much time that I told him, 'Don't worry. We have time. Let's get a coffee first.' And we were talking about everything: the Euros, the possible move to City. The time passed and I realised it was time to go. I went downstairs, but the plane had gone already. I was confused. How had I missed it? Had it taken off early? Which is when I realised I was still on French time and hadn't switched my watch to Moscow time.

As I watched the plane fly off, I couldn't help but worry whether this would make a difference to negotiations. But the funny thing was, it actually helped us. At the airport in Ufa waiting for me were people from Zenit St Petersburg. They were offering FC Ufa more money for me, so of course the club wanted to accept their offer. My agent said to the Ufa guys that I wasn't going to move to Zenit, that it wasn't about the money. 'We all know that you're going to get more from Zenit than from Manchester City,' he told them. 'But Alex is going to England.'

At that point, Ufa were expecting me to land two hours later to sort everything out. But my agent used the fact I had messed up and missed the plane to put them under pressure. He told them: 'Trust me, he's not flying to Ufa until you give us the green light to go to City. He's staying here until you agree.' So he turned this mistake into a negotiating tool! This detail changed everything. Who knows what would have happened had I flown there? Imagine if I had landed at the airport, completely alone, and had been met by the Zenit guys? I was 19, so maybe they could have persuaded me? It was like destiny, God's plan. Maybe it's not a random thing that I missed the flight.

In the end I flew to Ufa a few days later, when they finally realised I would only go to City and there was no other choice. I went there to say goodbye to everyone. They had a new manager and he was trying to convince me to stay, but I said: 'Look, put yourself in my position.

You have this one chance in your life, you have to use it.' Basically, he agreed with me.

I didn't really have a long chat with City before I signed. I didn't question anything, I just said yes, as you can imagine. You just want to join them. My agent and I flew to Madrid to sort out the visa and then travelled to Barcelona, where we met their lawyers. But then it was time for a medical. I was really worried I wouldn't pass. They send you into an MRI tube to check your entire body for hours; there was no way they would miss how bad my little toe looked. The bone had grown back together all crooked due to the pressure from the boots. To this day, it's much bigger than the one on the right. It's got a different colour – all red – and it doesn't look quite right.

After they had scanned my body for hours in the MRI, I was shaking a little bit from fear. I could already hear the doctor saying, 'Sorry, we cannot sign you, your toe is all wrong.' Because of that stupid toe, my transfer to Man City would fail. But eventually, everything was good. They were happy with everything, and I was ecstatic. I guess the one and a half months since I had broken it had given it enough time to heal, even with all the pain during games.

In the end, when we finally sat down again at a rooftop hotel bar, there was far less money on the table than we had been talking about, because of tax. But I said, 'I don't care,' because I wanted to follow the dream. I'm telling this story now because it might help young players and their families in the future. It's hard to negotiate when you're so desperate to join a club. The City lawyers said: 'Look, this is an academy player contract, right? As soon as you make your first official game for City, we're going to extend your contract with the real money that we pay full professionals. Not this academy player deal. So trust us.' Of course I said 'yes'. Follow the dream.

But do you know when my next contract came? The one that put me on full professional money? After I had played 43 games in the Premier League! I won two Premier League titles playing on an academy contract. That's where following the dream gets you. It was still good money for me, and certainly much more than I was getting in FC Ufa, but it was far from the wages of all the other players in my team. They were all world-class, so I expected them to be on more than me. But the main point here is that in football you cannot trust anyone's promise unless it's written down, signed and sealed. We should have written it into the deal that after one year, we would renegotiate. You can't rely on verbal assurances.

They did open negotiations with me when I just started to play regularly, but it wasn't until June 2019 that we finally agreed a new contract. I wouldn't say I deserved to extend my contract after my first season with the team in 2017-18, when I played only eight games in the Premier League and 14 games overall. I could accept that. But by 2018-19, I had played 29 games, 14 in the Premier League. So I'll never forget those words in that meeting in Barcelona: 'First official game – and then we're going to extend your contract.' This is the lesson for young players: follow your dream by all means, but be sure to get them to write down the dream's details in the contract.

City's scouting department later told me they had tracked me ever since that Arsenal game in the Youth Champions League when I was 17. I had no idea. Another English club had also been impressed, as it happens. But that's a story for later. I remember the first day at the Etihad training ground, shaking hands with Pep as he welcomed me. It was like being in a movie. 'Pinch me, please, maybe I'm still sleeping and dreaming.' His Barcelona team was one of the best in football history.

In the first training session, it was mainly reserves involved. Most of the international players had their vacations extended because of the Euros or Copa América. There were players who had come back from loans, some young players and just a few from the first team. The first guy I talked to in the dressing room was Bruno Zuculini, an Argentine midfielder who had just returned from a loan spell at AEK Athens – he told me the password for the Wi-Fi. This group of rather varied talents was never going to provide significant parts of the starting XI, yet training couldn't have been more serious. Every exercise was so sharp, so fast. It was another level, a completely different pace with and without the ball to anything I had experienced.

It was a tough intensity because it was pre-season. Most of the days were double sessions and the level was so high. I started to really enjoy it but, of course, I was tired. I could feel the fatigue in my muscles, because I had never worked in this way, in this rhythm and at this pace. I slept like a baby during the first night. But I knew this was the level I needed to be at and that I had to survive and then try to thrive in it. And I had to learn quickly. In the first few weeks we were flying to Munich for a pre-season friendly against Bayern. Because so many players were still away, I was in the starting line-up in midfield alongside Fernandinho and Fernando.

So my first game for City pre-season against Bayern Munich is in the Allianz Arena alongside two Brazilian stars. It felt like I was caught up in a whirlwind. It seemed impossible. Everything was moving so fast. It was also the first game for Pep as City manager and for his replacement at Bayern Munich, Carlo Ancelotti. And this is when I was first introduced to the personality of Pep. We had a long meeting before the game. I mean really long. And then we got to the dressing room. Guess how long we had until the warm-up? Fifteen minutes! Can you imagine this? The team arrives at the dressing room and has 15 minutes to change, get treatment, do their activation and go on the pitch. Usually, you arrive about 75 minutes to an hour before a game.

And then Lorenzo Buenaventura, the fitness coach who works with Pep, told us this was mild by Pep's standards, that once at Bayern the meeting had gone on so long, they came to the stadium seven minutes before the warm-up! And that was a Bundesliga game, not a friendly. Crazy, no? But because he's focusing so much on the football, he gets caught up in it.

IN BUT OUT

That day in Munich, Bayern played a very strong side because the Bundesliga started a bit earlier than the Premier League. And Carlo Ancelotti had just replaced Pep, so he must have been desperate to win. So against us in midfield were Xabi Alonso, Philipp Lahm and David Alaba. What a start! For the first 45 minutes, I touched the ball twice. Once from the kick-off and the other touch after we conceded, also from the kick-off. It was a joke! The level was way too high for me. With Lahm, it looks like you can get close to him, but as soon as you come near, he just gives the ball to someone. And his neck is always turning, he's looking around, scanning everything. I couldn't get near him, nor Alonso. Anyway, they won 1-0.

Even the pace of pre-season training was incredible. Everyone was working with the ball so well. It was as though I was lost in space, just floating around, unable to keep up. And these were the loan players and reserves. When the likes of Kevin De Bruyne, David Silva, Yaya Touré and Vincent Kompany came back, wow! The best in the world already and I am with them! It was beyond a dream for me.

Anatoliy came with me to England and helped me settle. I didn't speak a lot of English, but I got by, thanks to my mum. When I was in primary school, she paid a tutor to teach me English, and we had lessons once a week. She believed it would help me later in life. She was right. I struggled more with physical demands at City. Each day after the training session, I came back like a zombie, unable to speak or do much. I would just watch a bit of TV or listen to music in Ukrainian because I wasn't able to process anything more complicated. My brain needed a rest.

But I picked up the language soon enough. I only took two or three of the lessons City put on; I practised with my team-mates instead. Talking on the pitch. Talking in the dressing room. Talking while playing cards on the bus. Talking non-stop, basically. People say you can best learn languages by watching films, but in my experience, there's no substitute for talking. Real people sound very different to those in the movies. Especially in Manchester. If you don't talk and develop an ear for the way people around you speak, it's going to take you forever to feel comfortable talking.

Another piece of advice I would give: don't worry about making mistakes. Don't be timid. Just say what you want to say and ask people to correct. That's how I did it. A lot of people were laughing about my English at the beginning. Some are still laughing, because of my accent. I don't care. That's never bothered me. I also learned a bit of Spanish, by the way, because I thought it would help me communicate with Pep and a few of my team-mates.

Some players who come over from South America or warmer countries like Spain can struggle with the food and lifestyle, but I found England not too different from home on either count. Driving on the left – not really a problem. The biggest cultural shock for me was English humour. There's just nothing off limits here. To make jokes about your own family members in their presence is one thing. But to joke about a team-mate's mother, sister or brother? And everyone's laughing together? I found that weird. You would have never done it in Ukraine, for fear of offending someone.

Vinny [Kompany] was helpful right from the start. I remember in that pre-season we had a session at the Etihad and, at the end, a few of us were doing some two-touch shooting practice on the edge of the box. Vinny came over and said: 'How many of you are there? Seven? Right, I'm with the keeper, you all take shots and we'll see how many you can score against us.' So he speaks to the keeper and then sets himself up as this one-man wall, ten yards from us, and tells us to start shooting. Normally, when someone is shooting that hard, defenders just hide, turn away from the ball, especially in training. But he was jumping up, heading the ball away, getting his body in the way of shots, taking the full force of the strike on his chest and deflecting the ball away. And this is after a full training session, a guy who is 31 years old, a family man with three kids at home, a club legend. And he was taking time out to play with us! Not just playing, but demonstrating what was required at this club. It was the best example for any young players. 'Don't turn away from the ball, no matter what!' Fucking unbelievable. I had never seen anything like this in my life. Crazy, but at the same time, inspiring. He wanted to show us the commitment needed to succeed there.

As the first-team players returned, there was talk at the club as to what would be best for me. The decision would come down to me and Pep. A few days before, we were talking inside his office and he said: 'Alex, look, you are still young. And today I need players who are going to travel with me tomorrow to play semi-final Champions League against Real Madrid in the Santiago Bernabéu. Are you ready for it?' It was a rhetorical question. It was obvious I wasn't ready at that moment, which is how the move to PSV Eindhoven, where Phillip Cocu was manager, came about. But after the last training session I did with City that summer, when the loan to PSV had been sorted, Pep came to me on the pitch and said: 'Alex, I'm going to miss you.' That meant a lot to me.

The stint at PSV didn't turn out as we had all hoped, but I had made another mistake at the start of my City career also due to my eagerness to impress and follow my dream. After the Euros, I had no holiday. I flew from Paris to Moscow to Ufa to Madrid and to Barcelona, sorting out the move. I did the medical there in Barcelona and then went to Madrid to sort out my work permit at the UK consulate. I had that broken toe at the end of the season before and played in the Euros with injections. Mentally, there was the stress of all the negotiations between FC Ufa and my agent. And I had to move to this new city abroad to join a new team at a much, much higher level than before with just three days off before pre-season. I wish someone had said to me: 'Alex, that was a tough season. Take a break.' But I did the pre-season with City and then went on loan to PSV. As soon as I arrived in Eindhoven, I was gone again. Andriy Shevchenko, the new national team manager, called me up for a World Cup qualifier against Iceland.

They say 'Never meet your heroes', but meeting Shevchenko was one of the best things that ever happened to me. First of all, he's my idol. My generation grew up watching his games; we all supported AC Milan when he was playing there. And here I was, a few years later, getting coached by him, a former Ballon d'Or winner. You were bound to learn a thing or two.

Shevchenko is a very calm guy, but you can sense tons of steel under that smooth surface. He gave me one of the most important pieces of advice I ever received. 'Alex, listen to me,' he used to say. 'Play to your strengths, not your weaknesses.' It's simple but very deep and really made me think about my game. I cannot dribble past two or three players. I cannot outsprint superfast defenders to overlap my winger. 'So don't do it, Alex. Firstly, you will look silly. Secondly, you won't help your team. Thirdly, you will be disappointed with yourself. But don't be. Know what you're good at. Focus on that.'

Take Busquets. Was he dribbling past players under Pep? Was he tasked to run inside the box and finish the move with a shot? No. He was doing what he did, and he did it better than anyone else in that role. He built connections. He was always open to receive a pass. He always provided solutions for his team-mates. He controlled his position. He controlled the situation on the pitch. He controlled everything.

Shevchenko made me understand where I was as a player and where I should be. He gave me a road map to my own game. And he stuck with me. From his first game in charge in autumn 2016 until his resignation nearly five years later, he kept calling me up, whether I was playing well, badly or hardly at all for my club. Reporters and experts liked to grill him during every international break. 'Why have you picked Zinchenko again? Aren't you worried about Zinchenko's form? Can you trust Zinchenko, a player who's not starting for his club, for such an important game for the national team?' That debate went on and on. Shevchenko didn't care.

I'm sure it would have been a different story if my passport had a different colour. As an English or French player on the fringes of the first team at City, my national team manager wouldn't have kept capping me. I would have had to move clubs to get a shot at the national team. But Shevchenko believed in me. He supported me. Every time I joined up with the national team, I felt validated as a player. Without his backing, I would never have had the confidence to represent my country. He also had an amazing staff with him and our team improved a lot as a consequence. Results were good too: between November 2017 and September 2020, we lost only one out of 22 matches. It was amazing to be a part of that.

But my first game under Shevchenko didn't go according to plan. We only drew 1-1 with Iceland. Worse than that, I damaged the medial collateral ligament in my knee in training, but played anyway, with an injection, which made it worse. In middle of the action, when the adrenaline is flooding your system, you don't feel it much. But after, it's a horrible pain. I missed the first month at PSV and didn't make my debut until October. That didn't really help with settling in. Nobody likes a loan player who arrives injured at his new club.

I made plenty of mistakes as well at PSV. Firstly, in terms of my relationship with the manager, Cocu. It was one of those difficult situations because I heard a rumour the sporting director wanted me but the manager didn't. Obviously, I didn't know that when I moved. I only found out later from people at the club. But I still could have approached it better. The manager was obviously older than me, more experienced, and he would have seen many more players like me at 19. And he knew how to deal with them. Maybe I could have adapted better to him.

I don't really know why it didn't work out, but I'm not going to blame anyone. I always look at myself first, because it's so easy to point fingers at others. 'Ah, it's him, it's not me. I am the best. This is his problem.' You hear that a lot in football. No! If something doesn't work for you, that means you're not doing something right. I could have done better when I did get my chance, especially in terms of taking key scoring opportunities on the pitch. I should have scored more, especially in the first games. But it's also true that the injury and the fact I wasn't the manager's choice didn't help. Then, as a manager, you put this young player on for his first few games, he misses a lot of chances and the team is dropping points. Of course, you're going to play someone else. Which is what happened. I was on the bench until November, just coming on occasionally before making my first start.

Even so, there were good things about the experience. It was still a step up, completely different to Ukraine or Russia, and an amazing competition for young players to prove themselves and show their worth. The Dutch play very open football, the stadiums were always full and the teams had very young players, so you can compete.

There were some great experiences, especially in the Champions League. I made my Champions League debut against Bayern Munich at the Allianz Arena, a special ground for me after making my City debut there. It went as well as my first game, which is to say: not great. We were 3-1 down with about ten minutes to go when I got the sign that I would come on as a sub. The problem was, the home side kept the ball so well that there was no break in play to make the change. I stood next to Bayern's Javi Martínez, who also watched on impatiently. Four minutes passed, then five, then six, then seven. An eternity. I said to Martínez, 'Can you speak to your friends, please, so that we can come on?' He laughed. We both finally entered the pitch when play stopped in the 85th minute. Bayern had scored a fourth.

A couple of weeks later, Cocu picked me to start away to Atlético Madrid in their stadium. I was gathering experience, but I couldn't make much of an impression on the team. By the second half of the season, the manager didn't even put me on during games any more. He preferred bringing on players from the second team. For me, that was a big signal. He really didn't trust me. So I went to the coaching staff and asked to play for the youth team, because I still wanted to play 90 minutes each week. I said: 'Let me go to play for the Under-21s, Jong PSV, because I need some minutes.' And the manager was fine with that. So for the second half of the season I was playing in the academy league for Jong PSV. I even did some extra training sessions with an amateur team that one of my friends from Ukraine played in; I was that desperate for football. It was a strange time. Even some of the PSV players couldn't understand why I wasn't playing.

Could I have done more to force myself into the team? I've asked myself that question a few times. I don't think my attitude in training was lacking. Every single session without fail, I was the first one out and the last one in. I did plenty of extra work on the side. Maybe my body language could have been better. Looking back, I think my face wasn't right a few times.

Being a loan player is completely different to being signed to a club. In the latter case, you're an asset to your club, they will nurture you and have patience. As a loanee, you're just passing through. Once, I was in a rush to leave the training ground because I had an English lesson lined up. I wanted to improve my language skills before I returned to England. But the manager wanted to talk to me and said, 'Where are you going? What's the rush?' I told him I had to go to an English lesson. 'English?' he asked, raising an eyebrow. Maybe he would have preferred me taking Dutch lessons, I'm not sure. But I remember thinking, 'I shouldn't have told him that.' All the pre-match meetings and video analysis sessions were in Dutch, you see. One of the coaching staff used to come over to translate them to me separately. Cocu must have thought, 'If this guy is learning English rather than Dutch, he can't be very focused on the games here. He's probably thinking about Manchester all the time.'

It wasn't a very productive time but, even so, moving to new cultures always opens your mind. And in the Netherlands, the biggest shock to me was the fact that everyone can sauna together naked! Men and women! That wouldn't be possible in Ukraine. When I tell them about this back home, they're aghast. They can't understand it. It's strange when you see a seven-year-old, his mum, his grandmother, grandfather all together in the sauna naked. But it's just what you're used to and how you're brought up. As I said, you're learning new things every day!

And going there taught me resilience. I still respect all the people at PSV, because they dealt with me as I suppose I should have expected, and it was ultimately an amazing lesson that made me stronger. I learned how to deal with disappointment. After a game in which I hadn't played, I didn't know what to do with my emotions. But I didn't smash up the room at my apartment, though I felt like it. Instead, I would take myself into the woods and go for a run, just to get rid of all that energy and emotion. And then I'd come home, sleep and shower. It was tough, but I was still learning.

But then, in PSV's last game of the season, the team were already third in the Eredivisie and we couldn't go any higher or lower. The pressure was off. We were playing against PEC Zwolle at home and losing 1-0 at half-time. It was the last game of the season, everyone knew that I was leaving, so Cocu gave me a chance. Maybe he wanted me to prove myself in the second half when we were losing. So, second half, we beat them 4-1. I played 45 minutes, made two assists and finally played a good game.

After that game, we didn't go on holiday straight away but had an open training session for fans the next day. It wasn't serious training. We did a lot of exercise stations, where we would split into teams and compete, so that it was enjoyable for the fans to watch. And when it was over, the manager, Cocu, called me for a chat. We spoke for maybe 20 minutes and, after everything that had happened, he said, 'I would like you to stay for the next season. I promise you that the next season will be completely different for you. I really want you to stay here.' But I already made up my mind months ago, and I just said: 'Look, Mister, I already made my decision. Thanks for everything. But I'm leaving.' The odds were clearly stacked against me, but I wanted to give playing for City at least one more shot.

Back in the UK after the summer break, I started the 2017-18 pre-season with City unsure of my prospects. I couldn't have imagined how it was going to end, but that was a distant dream at that point. Think about it: City buy you. They send you on loan. The loan doesn't work out.

'This guy didn't play for half of the season for the first team. He used to play for Under-21s. We're not going to keep him for next season, right?' So what's the next step? Another loan, maybe? If you're lucky.

My dream was still to stay at City and play for them, not just be offloaded to other clubs. But it seemed unlikely. I thought I had more of a chance to stay and fight for a place in the first season, when Pep had just arrived, because the squad was thin then. In 2016-17, Alex Kolarov had to play centre-back at times, Fernandinho played left-back against Monaco. But when I came back from PSV, they had just bought Kyle Walker, Benjamin Mendy and Danilo. Then Aymeric Laporte came in January. So straight away, three full-backs, a midfielder and a centre-half who could play that position as well! But still, I wanted to stay there because the level was so high and I thought this was the place I could test myself, improve and learn for at least a year.

The club had other ideas. They really wanted to sell me and started negotiations with Real Betis and Wolverhampton. But it was like FC Ufa all over again. City wanted to sell me to Wolves. I remember even being in the canteen at the training ground and there was a Sky reporter saying: 'Wolves are expecting Oleksandr Zinchenko to join today.' I was eating lunch with the guys and everyone was laughing, saying: 'Alex, shouldn't you be on your way to Wolverhampton?'

But if I was going to move, I wanted it to be Real Betis, because they wanted me to play in midfield. My agents were in Seville and the move was more or less done. But it didn't happen because City preferred the offer from Wolves. You could see it, you could sense it, you can read the situation, because any transfers are a game. Every conversation in the office, they try to convince you. They will try to do what they want, not what you want. In the end, if everyone is happy, then the deal is done. But not in my case. I was so invested in Betis, I didn't think about Wolves. I was pushing them to let me go to Betis, because in my imagination I already had one foot in Spain.

I remember this chat with Txiki Begiristain, the director of football, when I asked him, 'Boss, how's it going?' He was always telling me: 'We're literally there. Give me 48 hours, give me 24 hours.' But in the end, the transfer window was closed in Europe but still open in the UK for a few hours. I think they were trying to delay it, to force my hand. 'Look, there are no other options, you have to go to Wolves.' They thought: 'If Betis can't happen, he will join Wolves for sure because he's not going to sit around for a year at City not playing?' Nothing against Wolves, but I didn't really want to join them, simple as that. In choosing Betis, I was opting for the football I wanted to play and a team I wanted to join. But in the end, the Spanish deadline passed, they didn't sign me, but I didn't go to Wolves either.

Your mind starts racing; you wonder how it will be after that. I couldn't really expect to play after not getting in the PSV team. But I continued to train hard, like I always did. And then Pep came to me on the training ground after one of the sessions and said: 'Alex, I'm happy you're staying with us. I can see you as a left-back. You need to be more aggressive here and here, but if you can do that, you will have your chance. You will get minutes in the league. So keep working hard.'

This was a trigger for me, the opening I had waited for. I knew it was a once-in-a-lifetime chance. I was going to be with this team for at least four months, until the transfer window opened again in January. 'Okay, this is the beginning, Alex!' I said to myself. 'This is your opportunity. Don't mess it up! Take it!'

5

From Zero to 100

I was on my phone, minding my own business, when Vincent Kompany approached me, grabbed my shirt and hauled me up, pinning me against the dressing-room wall, in front of the whole team. 'Listen to me,' he said. 'I never want to see what I saw today in training again. Never! You understand?'

'But Vincent,' I started to reply. 'It's match day, I didn't want to hurt him…'

'I don't care. You never let someone win a challenge like that again. You never duck a tackle like that again. Because you've come here from Ukraine to fight for yourself, for your family, for your contract, in every fucking single action on the pitch. In training and in matches, you give your all. You kill everyone, if necessary. Even your team-mates in training. I don't care. Then, after, you come back from training and we're in here in the dressing room, fine. You can be gentle and polite to everyone if you want. But out there, I don't want to see this again. Do you hear me?'

There was only one answer to that. I was 21 years old, he was the great Vincent Kompany, the best defender in the Premier League. You didn't argue. Welcome to Manchester City.

My crime? It was the morning before the Shakhtar Donetsk Champions League game in September 2018. It was my second season playing for Manchester City. I got some games in the 2017-18 title win. I even had a Premier League winners' medal. But I still knew my place. I was very much the new kid on the team. Benjamin Mendy was the first-choice left-back. Next was Fabian Delph. I was third-choice left-back. You know where you sit in the pecking order when that's your role.

On the morning of the Shakhtar game in Manchester we did some light training and, at the end, the first team played the rest, just to run through some moves. Most footballers will know this kind of session: nothing aggressive, don't kill each other, just make sure you don't get injured. More importantly, if you're the third-choice left-back, make sure you don't injure anyone important. Especially not the new £60m record signing.

There was one moment in training when Riyad Mahrez, just arrived from Leicester City, and I had a 50/50 ball. Normally, I wouldn't worry. I would smash the player and try to take the ball. But, you know? The morning of a Champions League game? Against Mahrez? A £60m signing? I let him win the duel. Not for free, I would say, but I was quite gentle with him. And then we went to the dressing room and Vinny had his say. This advice, fucking hell! It stayed with me forever.

Vinny was an amazing guy, always ready to help you. It didn't matter who he trained against: kids, first-team players, he was always giving his best. He was smashing everybody. When coming back from injury, normally you take it easy. Not Vinny. He hit the session like he'd never been away, 100 per cent. I've never seen this from a player. He would hammer me every training session. The way he was smashing Raheem Sterling, oh my gosh! I'll never forget this. Every single tackle, he used to destroy everyone. It feels like he just doesn't care, he's doing his job. I'll be honest with you, it was really scary being close to him on the pitch. First of all, he's massive. He's so aggressive and he's non-stop in your head. He's a machine, an absolute machine. Can you imagine being a striker playing against Kompany, having this guy in your face, shouting every single second? Thank God I'm not a striker, that I never had to play against him.

His advice to me that day was so important. He opened my eyes to a lot of things. This was Manchester City. You weren't allowed to let standards drop. Not even the third-choice left-back. Starting to train and play with these players and Pep was like doing a Windows or Apple software upgrade on your PC or Mac: a reboot, taking you to another level.

There was a Champions League game in the previous season, 2017-18, that showed me how far Pep was ahead of the competition. I wasn't playing at that stage, but it was against Napoli at home. Pep had told Fabian Delph, the left-back, to go inside into midfield. So we had a back three and two holding midfield players for the build-up. José Callejón was playing right wing for Napoli and I felt really sorry for him; he just didn't know where he was on the pitch when we had possession. Whom should he mark? 'If I go with Delph in the middle, then I create space for Leroy Sané and my full-back is exposed. So I need to be more here, but now we're outnumbered in midfield. So I go to Delph, but he just gives the ball to someone else!' It was like you could see his head spinning with confusion. Nothing personal about him. He's such an amazing player. But Pep does this to opposition players. That's when I was like: 'Wow, this is not football! This is chess!' I remember City destroyed Napoli in that game, not in terms of the result, which was 2-1. But in terms of the game: Napoli couldn't get close.

I watched Delph very closely. He was, like me, a central midfielder by trade who had been converted into an 'inverted' or 'false' left-back who took up a central position in possession. Looking back now, some of my advice to young footballers would be, don't do what I did. With the benefit of Pep and Vinny's advice, I would approach it differently. I had that chat with Pep in pre-season, August 2017, when he said he could use me as a left-back. Like always, I trained as hard as anyone. I showed my commitment to the team.

I also started to understand much more about this position, talking to team-mates, talking to Pep, listening to Pep, talking to the coaching staff. I had come as a midfielder and had only ever played a few games as left-back. The hardest thing was where you were in relation to the ball. What I realised as a full-back was that your position without the ball is the most important part of your game. More than your position on the ball. And especially when the ball is on the other side of the pitch. When the ball is on the other wing, straight away you have to think about: 1) Where is the ball? 2) Where is my opponent? 3) Where is the touchline? 4) What is the gap between me and my centre-back, in case someone runs in between? Because the priority is always to protect the inside.

Ball, opponent, line, centre-back: everything at the same time. As soon as I see the guy is starting to run behind me, I don't care about the gap to the touchline, I don't care about pressing. The opponent's ready to play a long ball and I see this guy starting to run? Switch on! Go!

Pep had promised me I would get a chance in 2017-18 and I believed him. And when the Carabao Cup comes around, that's when the young players start to get excited and are hoping for some game time. Benjamin Mendy had done his cruciate ligament in September 2017, so suddenly I was a little higher in the hierarchy. Fabian Delph was the first choice and I was now second choice. And sure enough, we played Wolves, then in the Championship, in the Carabao Cup in October and I was in the team. Left-back, like he said. My competitive debut for Manchester City. I played 120 minutes, ran 15 kilometres, and we won on penalties. Claudio Bravo was the hero, saving two, with Sergio Agüero scoring the winning penalty with a Panenka. But it was a tough game and a pretty shaky start to my City career. I was far from the finished article, especially defensively. They would go up that season as Championship winners and were already at Premier League level.

And my mistake? For years I had been waiting for his chance, fighting to make the squad list at a top club. It was my dream. Finally you get your chance and you're in the first team. What's the most normal emotion in the world? Fear. 'Don't mess this up! Don't make yourself look stupid. Just do the simple things well.' So you end up scared to make mistakes. You're not brave enough. In your head you're thinking, 'I waited years for this: one mistake and I'm finished. Don't take stupid risks.' And so it starts. You play simple, pass to the closest player, try to bed yourself in. This is the biggest mistake of every young player. I know it's natural, but now I say to the young players at Arsenal who start to play for the first team, 'Don't make my mistake.'

Trust me, every manager and fan can smell it, 'Ah, this guy, he's scared. He's not ready yet.' That is the first thing on their mind. But when I see young players seize the ball, taking risks, trying to dribble, even if they fail, I think: 'Fuck, this guy, he's crazy! He really thinks he's that good. If he has two options, he wants to take the hard one and do something for the team.' They are the players who grab their place on the team. They show they deserve to be on the pitch. But when you get scared and play within yourself, it doesn't work. You got to where you are by taking risks, so don't change when the stakes are higher. Be brave, even if this is your last chance this season. Even if you lose the ball nine times out of ten while trying to make a difficult pass to someone or dribbling past someone, no problem: next time you will understand how to do it. But if you're not going to even try, then you will never understand. I didn't do this at all. For too long at City, I played this safe football: no risk, simple, no mistakes. I was intimidated.

After the Wolves game I was back to my role as reserve left-back. Train hard, fit in, try to be useful. But I was making at least some impression, even if it was only in the gym. We played Huddersfield at the end of November. I was on the bench but didn't get on during the game. When we got back to Manchester that Sunday night, I didn't wait until the next day but went in for a late-night gym session. If you haven't played, it's important to work out, but most players will do that in a special training session the next morning.

Pep had noticed my extra effort, because a few days later he name-checked me. 'On Sunday night after the game, Alex stayed to train in the gym alone,' he said. 'That means a lot to me, because sooner or later he knows we are going to need him. He is a talented player. The way he plays, his decisions are always perfect. As a young player,

I hope in the future he will help us. He is going to stay for the whole season with us because I have the feeling we are going to use him.'

That's a huge boost to a young player and Pep knows exactly how to keep you engaged, even when you're not playing. Once in a training session, my team lost the ball. Although I was a winger, I started to sprint back with the player carrying the ball. It was not my player, because he was a midfielder. My player was the full-back, but I tracked him. Pep was reviewing training on the video later and stopped the image. 'Look!' he said, pointing at me to the whole team. 'That's what I like, that's what I need.' All these small things, he started to say what he likes, what he doesn't like. It was still only his second season, and a lot of us were new to his methods. Quickly you get his ideas, but it was a lot of information. The main players, even after one season, knew everything. They were like a machine. They were exactly where they needed to be positionally. It was like clockwork.

Later Pep would say: 'What I like the most about Alex was that, in the first years, we wanted to move him from here because we thought he wasn't going to play much and he said, "No, no, no. I'm going to fight for this position." I said, "Alex, it's difficult because we have many players in your position." But he said: "No, no, no. I'm going to play here." He trained really well. He never had a bad face. Even when he was playing sparingly, he always had good behaviour. Normally when you don't play, you can see it in the players' eyes. He was completely the opposite, still working extra time in the gym. Then he took the opportunity like it was the last chance in the world. That is a good football player.'

Maybe that's why he then gave me my next big moment, in December, my Premier League debut. Admittedly it was against Swansea, who had lost seven of their last nine games and were destined for relegation. And we were 3-0 up already when I got the signal from the bench to warm up and go on after 73 minutes. It must have been the least amount of jeopardy possible in a Premier League game. But it was an important milestone. I had come to England to play in the Premier League and now I had done so, even if only for 17 minutes.

And Pep was true to his word. That period at Christmas and New Year is another opportunity for young players; the schedule is so busy. We had Carabao Cup quarter-finals on 19 December, the FA Cup third round in early January and the two legs of the Carabao Cup semi-final against Bristol City on 9 and 23 January. All that and four Premier League games in ten days, trying to win the title.

Those cup games are perfect for young players. Obviously the FA Cup third round is usually when senior players are rested, and a semi-final against Bristol City, who were in the Championship, is a game Manchester City should win. So I knew there would be some opportunities. I didn't know I was about to become a cup specialist. I started in the Carabao Cup against Leicester, which we won on penalties. That was a young team with Phil Foden, Brahim Díaz and Tosin Adarabioyo, and I played for 120 minutes. My opponent for just under an hour was Riyad Mahrez, one of the best wingers in the Premier League. Frightening. But I just about held my own, despite picking up a little muscle injury in the second half. I didn't let it show.

When I started again against Burnley in the FA Cup third round, which we won 4-1, it was close to a full-strength team, with John Stones and Nicolás Otamendi as centre-halves and İlkay Gündoğan, Fernandinho and David Silva in midfield. That next Tuesday was the Carabao Cup semi-final first leg against Bristol City, and I started again at left-back, with Kevin De Bruyne, Yaya Touré and İlkay in midfield, with Raheem Sterling, Leroy Sané and Bernardo Silva in attack. This was getting serious.

I still had a lot to learn and it wasn't easy. But I was so lucky that I had an unbelievable circle of team-mates and coaching staff around me. Without them, it wouldn't be possible, because every single piece of advice from them was so important for me. I was like a kid with elephant ears and the eyes of a hawk, watching and listening to everything. How is this done? How should I train here? What position do I take there? How does this guy, with all his medals, do it?

Watching Pep coach was a revelation. I would have paid all my money to sit in on the coaching meeting, to listen to the conversations with his staff and understand why he was making certain decisions. As players, we only ever saw the outcome of his deliberations and his instructions, but not the process behind it. I would have loved to understand why he chose certain players over others in specific games, for example. He never explained why he picked or didn't pick a player. And I don't think a manager can do that. You don't have the time to explain your decisions to 25 people every three days, and even if you do, players will not accept it.

Kyle Walker told me about getting coached by André Villas-Boas at Spurs. He was 'an amazing person, and amazing guy, best friend to everyone,' Kyle said. 'But at some point, that closeness to the players was also a bit of his problem.' Because you have to put some players before others, and then you have a lot of heartbreaking situations. Every manager needs to work out their own style of man-management. Should you explain yourself all the time? Or should you just leave it and use your staff to keep everyone reasonably happy? Mikel Arteta was playing that role. He used to come and grab by you by the shoulder and have a word with the players on the bench: 'Everything is good, trust me.' And so on. He didn't say it to me at the time because I was so young and not in a position to deserve an explanation anyway. I was expected to put up and shut up, which I did. And honestly, I was just happy to learn from the others. There were top, top players in all these positions at City. In a squad of 25, I was the 25th.

Mikel was a bridge between the young players and Pep. He joined the club the same year as me, but I only really got to know him after my loan at PSV ended. It was obvious from the first minute that he was an amazing addition to a coaching staff that was already superb. The boys all loved him.

After every single session, Leroy Sané, Raheem Sterling, Gabriel Jesus, Bernardo Silva and I stayed behind for an extra half an hour with him. And he would have all these drills and games that I'd never seen before but which made you sharper and a better team player. It might be working on an action, such as a shot or a cross, but crucially not in situations where you are just standing still and rolling the ball, but in real-game situations.

For example, if I move to come inside into the middle area and receive the ball from my team-mate, Mikel would work on my first touch with the correct foot, getting the perfect angle, so then I can switch the ball to another angle. Then the next exercise could be that I receive the ball from somewhere wide, I play a one-two, cross, then come back inside, receive another ball and take a good touch. It was all game-specific situations. Most players who do extra work are just standing still or putting the ball on the edge of the 18-yard box and shooting from a standing position, just against the keeper. This is not even close to a free kick, because with a free kick you have a wall. This was different, dynamic and relevant to the real-game situations.

Mikel is a great human being and very relatable. We had lots of chats about the basics of football, the dos and don'ts, and also about my specific weaknesses, where I needed to improve. One of the best bits of advice he gave me was: 'Alex: speak on the pitch! You need to speak!' First, it keeps you in the game. You are fully focused. Then, any advice, any word can help your team-mate around you. And third one, it's so annoying! For your opponents, that is. Because when you play against someone, and they just talk, talk, talk, and you can see the vein on his neck popping out, you think: 'Fuck, this guy is ready. This guy wants to win. This guy is fully focused.' It disorientates the other team. Before that I was quiet, but Mikel helped me find my voice.

English football, I soon came to realise, feeds off noise. In Ukraine, we used to prepare for games by sitting silently in the dressing room, solemnly contemplating what might or might not happen. The bigger the game, the less people talked, out of deference to the occasion. It was different at City. The game started well before kick-off there, with loud music and players geeing each other up. I saw the difference it made. Players were switched on more when they entered the pitch. And their energy rubbed off on others, too.

Going back to Ukraine for national team service, I tried to pump up the volume in the dressing room. I talked a lot to players, urging them to be aggressive and get stuck in, but it felt a bit weird doing that in an otherwise quiet dressing room. They probably thought, 'Can this guy shut up already?' Everyone is different, I get that. Some players need silence to be alone with their own thoughts, some want to pray. But in general, the time at City taught me that you cannot have a silent dressing room before a game. If you don't want to speak, if you don't want to scream, if you don't want to switch yourself on and help others along the way, at least put on some good songs to get the blood flowing a little bit. I had never heard music in the dressing room before moving to England, but I would never go without now. Football is about emotions. It's to be enjoyed.

Mikel also did plenty of individual work with me – just me and him and someone else from the staff – on certain situations on the pitch. But most of the time he used to take us young players in a group and work with all of us. Mikel and Pep paid a lot of attention to every single pass, every control, the correct angle, the best foot to use to pass the ball. If you pass towards someone's weaker foot rather than the foot with which they're naturally receiving the ball, they need an extra touch. Then you're losing valuable time. It's so important for City and Arsenal that when you have the ball on one side of the pitch, you can bring all the opponents across, and then you can switch it. But when you do that, you don't want to waste your time on touches to bring the pass under control, because you need to use this opportunity to kill them with speed. And you as the receiving player have to be ready to adjust your position quickly. Pep and Mikel were across these minute details. I could feel myself growing as a player with them.

Pep always had the final decision on everything, especially tactics. He was also very hands-on in training, always watching, always teaching. There are head coaches who delegate everything to their assistants and then just silently observe from the touchline. That's not him. But like all good leaders, Pep surrounded himself with great people, and the way they pushed players to improve and achieve more was very much a team effort.

Mikel leaving a year later, in December 2019, was a big blow to me personally. I had to fight back the tears when he told me. Young players were going to miss him a lot, me in particular. In among that sadness we were happy for him, though. To go back as manager to the club you have captained must be a wonderful thing. Eighteen months earlier, when Arsenal were figuring out who Arsène Wenger's successor should be, we heard rumours some people at the club considered Mikel a better option than Unai Emery. I guess at the end, Emery was appointed because he had more experience. But there was no doubt Mikel was ready now. I think everyone at City had a strong suspicion that Arsenal would grow into serious rivals with him in charge before too long.

About that time I was starting to get recognised by fans – but not as myself. Everyone would call me 'Kev'. As in De Bruyne. I heard it all the time. When I was getting off the bus, fans were shouting: 'Kev, can I have a picture?' Then I would turn and they're like: 'Oh, it's not Kevin.' Maybe from afar we looked like twins, but when we are together, I don't think so. Anyway, I've always been better-looking than him.

Manchester can be a dangerous place to live as a young professional footballer, the club warned us. The legal department put on a two-hour seminar where they went through all the possible pitfalls that can await a single guy with a bit of money and a bit of fame. They told us to watch out for people trying to scam you and explained that there was a culture to sell 'kiss and tell' stories to the media. There was a lot of good advice for those prepared to listen. They really take care of you as a player in the Premier League in that respect.

If you've come here looking for salacious tales about wild parties with lots of girls, I will have to disappoint you. Firstly, I wasn't really in the market, because I always knew that I would marry a Ukrainian wife. I wanted to share my life with someone who had a similar background to me, who had the same values when it comes to raising children, family life and so on.

People see things differently. I would never say one way is better than the other. Never. And of course you can't help falling in love with a person, wherever they come from. But I wanted someone who understood our country's mentality. I'll give you an example. In Western Europe, it's quite common to have prenuptial agreements, especially for footballers and other people who are well off. For us Ukrainians, though, the thought of drawing up a contract that spells out what will happen and who will get what when the marriage fails, before you exchange vows, is totally weird. I can imagine how my wife would react if I told her after she said yes to my proposal that we would first have to talk about divorce. She would have said, 'Are you crazy? This is not a business proposition! This is either love or a job,' and told me to shove that prenup where the sun don't shine.

Would this be a good time to introduce you to my better half? I think so. You're in for a treat. The story of how Vlada and I became a couple is a very modern love story, featuring social media romance, plenty of missed opportunities, a botched proposal and…a fairytale ending.

We met when I was 14. More precisely, we didn't meet – not in person, anyway. She was one of the online contacts of a friend of mine on his VKontakte page, a Russian version of Facebook that lots of Ukrainians used at the time. I 'poked' her – I think that's the technical term – and we chatted for a while. But she lived in Vinnytsia, not far from the border to Moldova, 13 hours away by car. We never had a chance to see each other in real life.

We lost contact for three or four years, then found each other again, on Instagram. This time, we made a plan to meet in person. It was going to be during Euro 2016. She was in France with her family, I with the national team. She went to the game against Poland in Marseille but didn't tell me where she would sit, so I went off to the stand with the Ukrainian supporters looking for her after the game. And I found her. At last, we were eye to eye. I tried to give her my shirt, but some bloke tried to nick it. But she got it in the end. She took some pictures with it in the stadium and still has it to this day. We kept on talking but didn't manage to meet a second time. I went back to Russia to say goodbye to Ufa and then moved to Manchester, so we lost contact again.

At the time, she had a boyfriend and I had a girlfriend. I would see her from time to time back in Ukraine, hanging out with her friends, but it felt like the ship had sailed. But had it? We started talking again a couple of years later, her in Ukraine, I in Manchester. Then I said to myself, enough with all this talking and long-distance chatting. I need to seize this chance. 'Third time lucky' and so on. I invited her out on a proper date in Barcelona. I had a feeling from afar that she was the one for me. I was thinking about her all the time and felt so close to her. But after our rendezvous, I was certain. And then things happened very quickly. She visited me in England and I said, 'I don't want a long-distance relationship; I want you to move in with me.'

She was working for the main Ukrainian football channel as a sports reporter, a big job, travelling all the time for games, doing flash interviews on the touchline. But she chose me. She left her job for a different life in Manchester. I was totally convinced she was the girl I wanted to spend the rest of my days with. So, no more messing around. I had to marry her immediately.

The idea for the way I would propose to her came to me after Ukraine's 5-0 win over Serbia in Euro 2020 qualification. She was doing the game for TV and called me over for an interview. After, I kissed her. Nobody knew we were in a relationship at the time, and as she was quite the celebrity, it made a big wave. I thought, 'Let's do something similar. But this time with a ring.'

We played our last game against Portugal. A win would qualify us directly for the competition, while a draw would put us into play-offs. If we got either result, I would put the ring in my bag and present it to her live on camera. The whole of Ukraine would talk about it and we would have a nice memento for the kids one day. I told the producer I was available for the interview, as long as we didn't lose.

And what can I tell you? We won, 2-1! I had the ring in my pocket. But...I got cold feet. Not because of her. Of course not. But in Ukraine, it's customary to ask for the parents' blessing before you propose. You couldn't do that by phone, naturally, only in person. They lived a couple of hours away by car and I just couldn't find the time in the run-up to such an important match to get away from the team. I told myself, 'You can't do it without speaking to her mother and father first.' So I didn't go ahead with it.

But I couldn't contain my emotions. Qualifying for the Euros and nearly getting betrothed on the same night made me slightly lose my mind. I crashed one of Vlada's interviews with another player to burst into song, celebrating Ukraine's win, and did the same in the studio a few minutes later. I was totally out of it, on a complete natural high. In the end, I proposed later that night. In my boxer shorts. I didn't go down on one knee either. It was pathetic, the worst proposal ever. I feel so sorry for her. To this day, I'm ashamed.

What happened was that we argued after arriving back at home. I can't even remember what it was about. At 3 a.m., I took the ring out and said: 'Do you want me or not?' In other words, I made her an offer she could definitely refuse. But somehow, I'm still not certain why, she said yes. I count myself lucky in a million ways, every single day. To make up for this shambolic overture, I had the Olympic stadium filled with thousands of roses the next day and got down on my knees for the official photo of our engagement. And I promised Vlada she could have the best wedding ever, invite whoever and however many guests she wanted.

We got married on Ukraine's Independence Day, 24 August 2020. It was a lovely wedding but also the toughest day of my life. I got up at 7 a.m. to get ready for the photos. I wore this bow tie that was slightly too tight and restricted the flow of oxygen, so my head was throbbing like mad all evening. I didn't drink a drop of alcohol and hardly ate either, and we were up until 4 a.m. It was exhausting. But all the guests had a lovely time, which is what really mattered.

Before I got together with Vlada, I only ever went on dates in Ukraine in the off season. Manchester and its many nightlife delights didn't tempt me. I had also seen how the wrong kind of lifestyle can have a negative effect on your career. There were two Ukrainian players who were always making waves in social media thanks to their off-pitch antics, going to parties every week, wasting a lot of money, and always a big group of hangers-on around them. But in the end, they ran out of money, and all those 'friends' were suddenly gone, they didn't get any more 'likes' on social media, and they realised they had no one who was really close to them. You need to learn from those experiences and avoid them yourself. It's so important to have the right people around you, people who are genuine and smart, and who won't allow you to put yourself in silly situations.

Kyle Walker said it right. He told me, 'Look, as a footballer, you need to invest in yourself. If you need to have physio every day in your place, do it. If you need to have a pool in your place because swimming helps you, do it. Investing in yourself isn't cheap but it will pay dividends further down the line, because it will help you extend your footballing life and get you more contracts before this short career is done.'

We beat Bristol City over two legs in the Carabao and were now in a cup final. And now I was being used for Premier League games, starting against Newcastle, West Brom, Leicester and even stronger sides, such as Arsenal and Chelsea. Pep announced the first XI for the final at Wembley during the team meeting in the hotel and also named the substitutes, which was unusual. Standard procedure was for those who didn't start to find out whether they were in squad only in the dressing room in the stadium, when they either saw a shirt with their name outside their locker or not. But in this case, Pep wanted everyone to know up front because those who were in the squad would receive a medal at the end.

Danilo started as left-back. Pep preferred experience. I can't blame him. For me, being on the bench for that game was a huge achievement in itself at the time. A final at Wembley! I had only ever seen that stadium on television, the first time when Ukraine played there in the 2014 World Cup qualifiers. Yevhen Konoplyanka scored the opener and England needed a late Frank Lampard penalty to snatch a point. I never thought I might one day play in that famous ground myself. But here I was. I had progressed much more in six months than I could have possibly imagined.

We won the game comfortably, 3-0, the first of four League Cup finals that went our way in five years. City were so consistent in that competition. We joked that we could book the hotel a year in advance. Why were we so good at winning that specific cup? It's quite easy to explain. Firstly, the Carabao Cup is a competition where most of the big teams will give youngsters and fringe pros a run-out, at least in the early rounds. At City, even the second- or third-choice players were so strong that we beat senior teams from lower leagues or even our Premier League competitors, more often than not.

Secondly, Pep approached every game with the same seriousness and depth of preparation. It didn't matter if you were lining up in a friendly, the Champions League or in the second round of the Carabao Cup on a wet Tuesday in West Bromwich, you would receive the same detailed breakdown of your opponents' strengths and weaknesses, and precise instructions on how to play against them. Pep's attitude was, 'We respect every opposition.' By not changing his pre-match routine, even against sides from Division III or IV, he ensured the team's focus was always sharp. In football, as we have seen all too often, everything can happen. You need to be ready.

A title is a title and something to be cherished. But the timing of the Carabao Cup final, in late February, always made for the shortest of celebrations. You would meet friends and family for a quick dinner, then go home and train the next day again. I don't remember the team having a day off after winning the League Cup – the schedule was so tight that we couldn't afford to put our feet up.

The Premier League was a different planet compared with the football I had experienced before. You have less time and space than everywhere else and more pressure. I'm not just talking about the game itself. If you don't give 100 per cent in training and prove that this is your spot, there are five guys behind you, ready to come and take it from you. You can score a goal in a game or make a wonderful assist, which might be enough to be untouchable for a while in some clubs, but it won't be in the Premier League. The internal competition is relentless.

For a while, I worried that I was too small, too skinny. All 1.75 m and 61 kg of me, coming up against these mountains of men in games, against these monsters. I asked myself, 'How can you deal with these guys? Do I need more muscle?' But I realised that playing in the Premier League wasn't all that different to the streets of Radomyshl in that respect: you can be skinny and small if you take your decision quicker. Look at Bernardo Silva. He's the tiniest guy. Mahrez is also skinny, but he's a magician. Both are among the most devastating players I have ever seen. If you are smart and read the game well, you can always be there.

It helps if you can run a bit, too. Riyad used to wind me up all the time, saying he was so much quicker than me. One day after training, I couldn't take him any more and challenged him to a race. He accepted. Kyle Walker acted as the ref but let Riyad get away with a false start. He had two metres on me, but I still finished first. Kyle, who had filmed the whole thing, was on the floor, laughing. I went with the video on my phone and showed it to everyone, in the dressing room, in the showers, in the treatment rooms where players were being massaged. I only stopped short of going into Pep's office with it. That argument was settled once and for all.

As the 2017-18 season reached a climax, I was a part of the team. Sort of. Perhaps the biggest game was the Champions League quarter-final against Liverpool. This was the year before we went head-to-head in the Premier League with them. Liverpool had yet to reach those heights, but Virgil van Dijk had just arrived that January and Sadio Mané, Mo Salah and Roberto Firmino were beginning to form the combination that would make them so powerful. That night at Anfield we were 3-0 down in 31 minutes and effectively lost the tie there. But the game is more remembered for the bus journey into Liverpool, which was something extraordinary, something you couldn't believe could be allowed to happen.

Stones were being hurled at our window. I looked to the side and caught a glimpse of a stone coming directly at me. I braced myself for impact. I thought it would smash the window and hit me. Luckily, the glass was reinforced and it bounced off, but there were cracks all over the windows. People were calling out: 'Guys, get back from the windows.' Everyone was crowding in the central aisle. By the time we got to Anfield, the bus was totally destroyed and the glass near the door was so damaged it was about to shatter. When we got to the dressing room, fear had turned into real anger. We were on fire. 'Let's smash them for everything they've done, the way they welcomed us,' people were saying. But it doesn't matter what you say. If they're better on the pitch, words mean nothing.

Liverpool killed us in transition that night. Pep's biggest fear was getting caught on the break. He used to say, 'The pitch has to be small. We cannot play in big spaces. We have small players. If the ground they need to cover becomes too big, we're dead.' That's why counter-pressing was so important for this team. Everyone needed to be in the right position to win the ball back high up the pitch the very second an attack broke down. The team are collectively too close to the opposition half – small pitch, remember? – to react in the traditional way, which is for everyone to fall back and defend the attack near your own box. Pep hates it when games open up like that, when it's up-and-down, old-school Premier League football, uncontrollable. His idea is to achieve total dominance over the ball and suffocate opponents. When I say, total dominance, I mean TOTAL DOMINANCE. We did it so well, opponents found it impossible to get out of their half. You had to have big balls to try to pass your way through this press. Very few teams were able to do that. But those who somehow managed to make ten to 15 passes against us would usually find a bit of space and get one or two chances. Easier said than done, though.

We always went out to score quickly, in the first 20 minutes. Maximum aggression, shock and awe, from kick-off. Most of our opponents tried to defend very deep against us, so the idea was to tear into them straight away, before they settled. Then, once you take the lead, they have to change tack and come out a bit, which they're mentally not really prepared for. That's the moment we would punch them twice, three times, four times in quick succession – and knock them out.

For those who didn't have the courage or the means to play through those waves and waves of pressure, the only option was to defend for their lives and somehow get into half-time at 0-0. We found that very frustrating. When you dominate teams but have nothing to show for it, you can get a little bit annoyed or nervous. Having played hundreds of games and watched thousands, the guys know that football has a nasty habit of kicking you where it hurts if you don't convert your superiority into goals. One set-piece, one counter-attack, and 89 minutes of control count for nothing. Dealing with such moments was incredibly hard, but on the relatively few occasions they happened, Pep and the players tried to learn from them and aim for an even higher state of perfection.

Our consolation after getting knocked out by Liverpool in the Champions League was the Premier League record of 100 points, something you can't imagine will be beaten for some time. It was all over in April, when Manchester United were beaten at home by West Brom. In the end, the gap to them was 19 points.

It was incredible to experience that, even if it felt as though I had won that title 'in my jeans', having played only eight matches. Still, the first title! You are champion of the Premier League and you have your medal, having played at least five games. It was hard to process. A year earlier, I had been begging for games in the PSV Under-21s. Now I was a small part of history, a part of the Premier League's best-ever team. It was unthinkable.

Critics and former players had told Pep he couldn't win the league playing his brand of passing football after City had finished third in 2016-17. He needed to change, they said, be more English, pay more attention to things like tackles and crosses, be more direct. He didn't change, though. He just needed a bit more time to perfect his formula. Watching their games from the Netherlands, I felt they were lacking a bit of depth. Fernandinho had to help out as left-back a few times. You could see in their defeat against Monaco in the last 16 of the Champions League that they were missing a few players in key positions for his grand vision to take shape. And they were also a bit unlucky with some results in the league. I had no doubt this team would come good: Pep was creating something unique.

All the doubters and pundits had to eat their words. Pep didn't just win the league: he destroyed it. It was 5-0 vs Liverpool, 6-0 vs Watford, 5-0 vs Crystal Palace, 7-2 vs Stoke City, 4-0 vs Swansea, 4-1 vs Tottenham, 4-0 vs Bournemouth, 5-1 vs Leicester City, 4-1 vs West Ham. We were out of sight, untouchable. The Premier League had never seen a team outclass the competition so thoroughly and probably never will again.

When you win the title at City, you celebrate properly. That first Premier League title I won, I got the call and they said, 'Alex, you have 40 minutes to go to the training ground because we are celebrating there already.' And you had to go there. It was compulsory. You cannot say, 'Oh, I have kids,' or 'I have something else on'. No, no, no, I had to go there. I went there. I was the last to arrive, and Pep was there with a big cigar in his hand. This was the first Premier League trophy for him as well. I promise you, I think we went to every restaurant in Manchester in the next few days. Incredible. I was almost too tired to celebrate. I don't really drink. I've never been in the position where I've lost my memory because of alcohol or where I have thrown up. Never. I've never been properly drunk. A little bit tipsy at best. I can have a few drinks, but never during the season. At that time, there was no chance of not joining in, but I didn't go overboard. As a young player, I felt I couldn't do that. I need to respect my body and my schedule as a professional. I don't touch alcohol at all during the season. If I had a normal job, I probably would get the odd beer in after a shift, but I can't arrive at training tired or do anything that affects my fitness. There are ten people behind me, just waiting to take my place.

We were celebrating for maybe four days. We went everywhere. The parades as well, across the city centre. Amazing feelings, incredible emotions. And Pep used to tell us: 'Guys, when you win, you celebrate. That's why we are living. That's why we have one life. You deserve it, and you need to celebrate it. And if you celebrate, celebrate properly. Otherwise, what are we living for?'

6

Treble Winners

When we came back for the 2018-19 season, we would face extraordinary challengers for our title in Liverpool. This was the season when no one seemed to lose. We would win on Saturday, they would win again on Sunday. They would play at 12.30 and win; we would play at 5.30 p.m. and win. Step by step, we matched each other.

But I was still fairly junior and mainly being used for cup games. Against Burton in the Carabao Cup semi-final (9-0), I scored my first goal for City, a shot into the top corner from outside the box. I wasn't really sure how to celebrate and ended up throwing an imaginary basketball for a three-pointer, don't ask me why. It was a moment of such intense joy that you're not quite yourself. The boys, in typical fashion, had a laugh though. 'You were trying to cross!' one or two were saying. The lack of respect. Of course I was trying to shoot! And what a fine shot it was, too.

I hadn't been named in the Champions League squad for the group stage in the previous season because City had probably expected me to leave that summer. I therefore missed out on a chance to play against my old club, Shakhtar, and travel to Kharkiv, where they were playing after the occupation of Donbas. It was a shame, because we had already qualified for the knockouts as group winners before the match in Ukraine, and Pep was rotating a lot, giving youngsters like Tosin Adarabioyo a run-out. Phil Foden played as left-back that night. I might have played. It was painful.

But the draw put us together in the same group once more a year later. This time, I thought I might get a game, especially when I was put up for the pre-match press conference in Kharkiv. Players who do the pressers usually start. But the next day, I wasn't even in the squad. I think I must have been the first player in the history of the competition who was put up before reporters but then left in the stands by the manager. Was it something I said? I don't think so.

Pep caught me in the hotel lobby before the team meeting and said, 'Alex, I'm sorry. Unfortunately you are the only player not in the squad today.' On the bus to the stadium, I couldn't hold back my tears. We were in Ukraine, playing against my old side. The whole stadium and all the media were eager to see how I was getting on at City. And then I was sat in the stands, while players who were younger than me were part of the squad. It was a very painful evening, and us winning 3-0 was not much of a consolation.

Pep realised how I felt and gave me a hug after the final whistle. He didn't apologise. He didn't have to – he's the manager. He can't worry about the feelings of every player. That's impossible. But I read that gesture as him saying: 'I've made a mistake.' I'm not sure why he didn't include me. He was probably so focused on the game, naming the right starting XI and having the right tactics that he didn't think about me. He's so intense and obsesses about football so much that he can forget to eat on match days. A young Ukrainian kid being sad about not being in the squad can't have been high on his list of priorities that night.

Two weeks later, for the return leg, my parents came to Manchester. My expectations were low. Mendy was fit and so was his back-up, Fabian Delph. I called my parents and said, 'We will probably go and watch the Under-19s together, but let me wait a bit and see who's in the squad.' Ten minutes later, my name was on the board. I don't know quite how, because all the senior players were available. The next day, I was perhaps extra careful in the training session not to get injured or to injure anyone. I got that earful I mentioned from Vinny in return. I learned my lesson. Even better, I played for 90 minutes and we won 6-0. During the game, we had just won a corner. Pep called me over and gave me a playful slap. 'Don't ever tell me that I don't play you against your former team,' he smiled. 'You play amazingly well. Keep going.' I hadn't said anything before – I wouldn't have dared. Someone else from the playing staff must have told him how much not featuring in the away game had hurt me.

I did get another chance to prove my worth in the Premier League, when we played away against Southampton. It was 0-0 and, as a full-back, I cut inside to receive the ball. But I was not well prepared for the pass, lost it and we conceded: 0-1 at Southampton on 37 minutes. Not good. We already knew we couldn't afford to lose any games this season. Thankfully, the team reacted well. We scored straight away, then a few minutes later, we scored another one, then, still in the first half, I made an assist to Sergio Agüero, he scored and now it was 3-1 at half-time. Crisis over.

At half-time Pep made an example of me, but not like you would expect. He said: 'Guys, learn from this young boy. Did you see when he lost the ball? He made a mistake, we conceded a goal. But look how he reacts. After his mistake, he was not hiding. He was asking for the ball again and again, in every single action. We all need to learn from this. This is how to react.' Even after the game, which we won 3-1, he was speaking to the press, saying: 'Alex was the best on the pitch, the way he reacted.'

But the kicker to that praise was that for next five Premier League games I was not in the squad! I sat in the stands. I didn't get an explanation. In my opinion, he didn't owe me one. And from what I heard from other players, he never explained his decisions. Never. So, in your head, you need to find this motivation to push yourself.

But the odd thing is, I would say I was probably really bad at recovering from mistakes. When I made a mistake, especially a big mistake that led to a goal, I would dwell on it. I might hold my head for ten seconds after or in a game. I could still be thinking of a mistake I made a few weeks ago. It's getting better with experience; you learn to push those thoughts aside. At one stage, I caught myself worrying so much, I told myself, 'You'll soon be bald if you carry on like that.' The ability to let bygones be bygones is a hugely underappreciated quality of footballers. We had a few like that in the squad, and watching their behaviour was a huge eye-opener for me.

On the very few occasions Mahrez had a bad game, for example, you would have never guessed it from his demeanour coming into training the next day. I would have thought about it, been in a bad mood. But he was laughing and his usual happy self. Fernandinho was the grand master, however, the absolute best. He would never show you that he made a mistake. If he missed a ball or lost it, his face never changed. He can just switch off disappointment in a game, delete his emotion. If he wasn't in a good moment, if his form dropped, if he wasn't playing well, and people were killing him, he just kept doing simple and basic things well.

And I learned a lot from Fernandinho. He was a superb role model. He told me the story about the day Brazil lost 7-1 in the 2014 World Cup semi-final to Germany, on home soil. This was the World Cup the whole nation was expecting and demanding them to win. After one of the goals Brazil conceded, Fernandinho ran into the goal and grabbed the net with his hands. He was inside the goal, holding the net in despair, head down. All the photographers took this picture. It went everywhere; it was the defining image of the defeat. All over social media, in every paper and magazine.

'Can you imagine how painful it was?' he told me. 'I was in such a big stress and eventually I realised I had only two choices. One, give up and just put your head down and don't play football any more. Or don't play at the highest level, just come back to the Brazilian league and finish there. Two, prove yourself at the highest level once again and show to the people that this was a complete one-off, one of those random things that can happen in football, but say nothing about your quality as a player. I chose this response.' He taught me that looking forward is the right way to deal with any setbacks. Because football gives you lots of chances to redeem yourself, very quickly.

That's why I don't give up and don't react badly to unsuccessful actions on the pitch or when I make mistakes now. And maybe Pep thought I did it well back then against Southampton. But it took me much longer to learn this. And I'm still nowhere near as cool today as Fernandinho and Mahrez were back then. I still have trouble getting big defeats out of my system.

İlkay Gündoğan and Kyle Walker were the most consistent players I've ever seen. We are all humans, sometimes we're in good form, sometimes in bad form. We're high and low. But these guys were always top-level. Their fever chart is a flat line, 9/10 every single game. A poor game for them was 8.5/10. They never dropped lower than that.

İlkay is super intelligent, an amazing professional and such a nice guy. He tore his anterior cruciate ligament in 2016, but four years later, he still did special exercises and treatment sessions after every training session, to go the extra mile and get game-ready. In five years, I never saw him leave the training ground early. This kind of commitment is the key to his consistency. He really looked after his body so well. In 2014, he had a really bad back injury that kept him out of the game for a long time. He was so desperate to find a cure, he even went to a hospital in Crimea for advice. In the end, he had surgery in Germany. They fixed him. But he still flew in a specialist from Germany to work with him on a regular basis, to maintain that fitness. He hardly missed a game.

There were big players everywhere you looked. Take David Silva. Off the pitch, he was really quiet and unassuming. Some players turn up in expensive clothes to training, but he came in the same jeans and the same Adidas trainers every day. He didn't do rousing speeches, he didn't motivate you by talking. He wasn't like Vinny, who screams at you every single second, for every single action, directing you like he's playing FIFA: Vinny holds the joystick, and he moves you in the right position with it. If you follow his words, you will play well. The more I played with him, the more I understood what I needed to do to belong in this team.

David Silva, by contrast, made everyone better without saying much. His ability spoke louder than any words. Of all the players I've ever had the pleasure to play alongside, his first touch was the best. Unreal. You can fire any ball at David Silva: high, low, bouncy, whatever. He always controlled it with a perfect first touch.

In December 2017, his son Mateo was born months prematurely. He was in an incubator for a long time, with many issues. Pep gave him permission to fly home as often as possible to be with his family during those difficult moments. He took a couple of weeks off over Christmas but then started to shuttle back and forth, just for the games. One day before the match, he was there to train with us. The next he played, then he flew straight back to Spain again. You'd expect his form to suffer. Lots of travelling, hardly any training, and all the worries about your child on top of that. But no, he was amazing. Every single game. Goals here, assists there, he even captained the side a few times as well. He became an even greater player, knowing what he was going through. What an unbelievable pro.

I will never forget the celebrations for the Premier League title and League Cup in 2018. After parading the bus through the city, we went to a stage in Deansgate. A few players were saying things, but then David Silva came up on the huge video screen with Mateo in his arms. The crowd went wild. Everybody had goosebumps. He had missed the last few matches – as we had sewn up the league championship – and gone home to Spain. He apologised for not being there – no apology necessary, obviously – and thanked the manager, the club and all the team for understanding his situation and having been so accommodating. Football can be a pretty tough business but, that day, we could all feel the love. Playing in a triangle with him and Leroy Sané on the left side was a special time. You could just give them the ball and know they would do something extraordinary with it.

Gundo, David Silva, Vinny, Fernandinho, they were among the best I ever played with – how they behaved, how they reacted when they were not playing. I tried to take something from all of them. Obviously most of the time they were playing, because they are fantastic footballers. But on the few occasions David or Dinho were not playing, they didn't show their emotions. They were working to the same level they always did. And that was a big lesson from top players. Even though they were the best players in the world in their position, sometimes they could be on the bench. But they didn't panic. And then you see some other players who get dropped and start to do bullshit training sessions: bad attitude, bad body language, saying negative things to the team. You learn from them all, what you should do and what you shouldn't.

And what about Nicolás Otamendi? This guy used to destroy everyone in the training sessions. Destroy them! And his English was still zero after seven years at the club. I used to be his best friend, other than Sergio Agüero. But without talking. Just through the body language. It was incredible. He was such a nice guy but would still destroy everyone in training. And nobody would whistle to rein him in! I think the worst job in the world is to be a referee at a City training session. No one wants to lose, and if you blow up, the players destroy you. No one from the staff wanted to be the referee. It was a nightmare for them.

Just watching Kevin De Bruyne play and train was incredible. I was joking with him that his body doesn't look like a footballer's, because he's rarely in the gym. But when he's on the pitch, he's extraordinary. He used to tell me, 'Don't worry, next game I will run more than anyone else – again!' And it's true, because he's so powerful in the lower body. His legs and especially his glutes, which take all the pressure and provide the power, are incredible.

To be honest, sometimes he doesn't seem special. He can make a simple mistake in training in the way that David Silva never does. Gündoğan never loses the ball. But Kevin, he can make mistakes in training. But then, in one moment, he does something so special that no other player can do. And all you can say is, 'Wow! That's Kevin!' In the game, the things he does are incredible. He was more like Sergio Agüero. In training sessions, they may seem as though they are not giving their all. But in the game, they are a different breed.

I'll also never forget Kevin's preparation for a game. For me, around 45 minutes before you go out to the warm-up, I start my routine. I get changed, get some treatment, massage, a muscle rub, start muscle activation in the gym. And I need to be focused, listening to music. Most of the guys are like me; they are so serious. But Kevin, he leaves his backpack, goes to the room where all the kit men are, has a chat and just talks. Then he will look at his watch and see it's ten minutes to warm-up and say to them: 'Oh, okay, another two minutes, and then I will go to change.' Then he just changes quickly, no treatments, nothing, straight on the pitch and he will do his thing.

Sergio can sit on his phone for 40 minutes, and five minutes before the warm-up, he starts to get changed and warm up. So you question yourself and think, 'Well, maybe my routine is not the most important thing.' But we are all different, and what you do in the game is what matters.

Kevin has this vision to play these passes, and his teammates know that he can give them the ball. So when he's on the ball, without any pressure, all the players start to make runs. If the centre-back receives the ball, maybe the attacking guys aren't going to bother to run in behind, because they are not trusting his ability to deliver that pass. But when it's Kevin, everyone is getting on their bikes!

All the time I was learning, from the players and from Pep. It was like an intense university seminar every day, except that you are not able to get this education at any university or online. You can watch the documentary or read the book, but being inside that kitchen at the very point at which he is cooking up the dish, that's where you really learn. Pep would explain so well where you needed to be, how you needed to receive the ball and where you needed to play it. His communication is so good that it makes your life much easier on the pitch.

If you explain it from just one perspective, only half the team is going to understand it. But when he explains it, position by position, everyone understands it. And then you can fly. I guess in the future, football will be even more like chess. Everyone will be so technical, so fast, so strong, it will all be about finding advantages by being in the right positions, in the right spot. That's what City are trying to do. They're always trying to find the advantage, especially in the final third, taking play to one side, moving the other team there and straight away switching it to the other side, where they have a guy in the 'pocket', the half-space between the touchline and the box, and the winger, who can both gang up on the opposition, two against one.

What is interesting is that Pep never shouts. It doesn't matter how we play. It doesn't matter what the result is. I don't remember him ever saying we didn't play well. Once, maybe. Every time during the half-time break he would say, 'Guys, fucking well done.' That's how he started his speech. Every single half-time. 'Bravo guys! Well done!' And then after, he would be, 'Look, here, here and here.' He used to say, 'Guys, as a player, you are much, much better than me. But trust me, I have a bit more experience in terms of coaching, and I've been in these positions already, so you can trust me in this case.' He always chose the right words.

At half-time, there are always six minutes where he doesn't speak at all. He gives us a break, to breathe. And then he just needs seven minutes of attention. He takes two boards in the dressing room and, while we are resting, he writes out our positions, where we should be. One board is defensive, the other board is offensive. And then his words, always the same: 'Guys you're fucking tough. You're fucking amazing.' Then it's: 'Listen, what we need to do, defensively here, we have a few problems. Offensively, guys, look where the spot is. Look at the area, look what they're trying to do.' It looks so simple, but it's right. That's what you need to do in the dressing room at half-time. I mean, it's simple to put up two boards, one defensive, the other offensive. And just give the team confidence, even if we were losing. If we play good or bad, he just always says: 'You played good.' He won't kill us. He wants to boost us, to lift us.

One of the reasons City were such a successful team was because they had at least two big players for every position who were ready to perform at the highest levels and deserved to play. That City machine was built to deal with all eventualities; it had so much quality in depth. Twenty-five unbelievable players who all deserve to play, who are trying to show the manager why they should get the nod. There were five-vs-two rondos that went on forever; none of the passes went astray. The guys in the middle had to be swapped around because they were so exhausted chasing shadows. The quality was a joke. As a manager, you see this and you get a massive headache. How do you choose when everyone is at such levels?

But one day, Pep had seen something he didn't like in training. There was no problem with the football – it was superb, as usual. But some players looked unhappy that they didn't get much game time. So he called a meeting and said, 'Guys, I can smell something is wrong here. Some of you have faces like you ate three lemons. I know sometimes you're not happy with my decisions. I know this. But I'm earning money for it. It's my job to make these decisions. I can be wrong 10,000 times. I can be right 10,000 times, I don't know. But I love you all. And I want to tell you a story.

'At Bayern, we played against Juventus in the Champions League in the last 16. I already knew my team, but I wasn't sure about one position: holding midfielder. Should I put Xabi Alonso or Arturo Vidal there? All my coaching staff said, "Put Vidal. He played at Juventus. He knows everyone." But I was still thinking about it. In the end, I decided to go with Xabi Alonso.

'In the dressing room, when we arrived at the stadium and I had already announced the line-up, I saw something I had never seen before. Vidal came over to sit close to Xabi Alonso. And he started to talk with him about the game, about this player, about that player, about all their weaknesses and strengths and the way Juventus played in midfield and so on, all way to warm-up, and then again all the way to kick-off. And I was like, "Fuck. Wow! This is the key to success. This is the right reaction."

'Usually, a player like that would be so disappointed. They would stare at their phone and not talk to anyone. But the opposite happened here. I need such players in my club. I need everyone to behave this way, supporting each other, helping each other. If everyone will do this, we will be so successful. We will be an unstoppable team. Trust me.'

This is coaching. Supporters and the media can only see the end product, good performances or bad performances. But they can't see how important the emotional mood inside the team is. If things aren't right there, you'll get bad results sooner or later.

I eventually saw some highlights from the game Pep talked about. Bayern destroyed Juventus on their own pitch; it was a miracle the game somehow ended 2-2. But Arturo Vidal started in midfield that night, not Xabi Alonso, so perhaps Pep had the story the wrong way round. But it doesn't really matter. He had noticed bad vibes creeping in from the players who were frustrated with sitting on the bench and he plucked out an example from his vast coaching experience with superstars to show us how crucial support and loyalty are. To care for your team-mates is not the natural state of affairs for professionals. They are always competing, first with themselves, then with the players in the team, then with opponents. But at some point you need to see the bigger picture and curb those instincts. If you sit on the bench full of resentment and secretly wish bad luck on your team-mate because he plays in the same position, if you rock up to training with a sour face each day, that negativity will spread like mould in a dirty bathroom. A team like that will never achieve big things.

It doesn't matter how good you are, you can only achieve big things if players come together and play not just with but for each other. Show me a side winning big things and I'll show you a side brimming with positive emotions, good spirit and the right mentality. I sat there, 20 years old, listening to those instructive tales from Pep featuring big football names I had grown up watching, and I think I got it. A light went on. After teaching men what had to happen on the pitch, he also made me understand what had to happen off it. The players around me were looking at the manager with big eyes, nodding, when he finished. That moment, everyone got it.

We lost some games at Christmas to Crystal Palace and Leicester and it looked as though Liverpool would get their chance. But after Boxing Day 2018, we won every game bar one to the end of the season in the Premier League. It was unbelievable. In the middle of all that, we won the Carabao Cup, and this time I started the game, played for 120 minutes and got my hands on the trophy. Chelsea managed to hold us to a goalless draw after extra time, but we won on penalties. I would have been sixth or seventh in line and felt happy to take one, but it didn't get to that. Chelsea fans and neutrals will remember the game because Chelsea goalkeeper Kepa Arrizabalaga refused to be subbed for Willy Caballero just before the spot kicks.

My life as a footballer was by now beyond anything I had ever expected. I was a player in the best team the Premier League had ever seen. I know full well I wasn't the greatest player or the most important guy in that team, but it was still incredible to be there and earn my place.

The Premier League title race was phenomenal. The lead changed between us and Liverpool 32 times! Pep never lost his cool, though. He stuck to his methodical approach and simply gave us the tools to succeed. Honestly, nerves never came into it for us.

Liverpool were leading into the home straight but had played a game more, and our catch-up game was against Leicester at home on 6 May. Win that and we went top and then had to win at Brighton to be sure to win the league. Drop points to Leicester and the title was in Liverpool's hands. Liverpool had Wolves at home on the last day and we knew they would win, whatever. And the Leicester game was hard. It was 0-0. There didn't seem to be any way to break through. Brendan Rodgers was the coach and they had beaten us earlier in the season. And that was when Vinny stepped up with his incredible goal, from 25 yards out, the most amazing strike. You can't imagine a centre-half scoring a goal like this. We knew that he was probably going to finish playing for City at the end of that season, that this was one of the last few games for him. There hadn't been an announcement, but we could sense it. And this was his parting gift to City. It decided the Premier League title.

But even so, playing Brighton at the Amex Stadium was one of the most memorable games for me. We knew that Liverpool were going to win. For three months, both teams had no draws. Just win, win, win. Before the game, Vinny came up with a rousing speech. 'You were the best in France, the best in Spain,' he said, pointing at players. 'You were born to do this! Everybody ended up here for a reason.'

We had practised defensive corners going into that game because we knew Brighton did two types of corners. Either they would have everyone starting from the penalty spot and then just run into position, and in this case my job was to stay on the front post. Or the second option, the one we practised dealing with most, was when everyone floods the six-yard box. In that case, I had to cover the last man at the far post.

But they went 1-0 up. From a corner. Everyone had started around the penalty spot, so I went for the first option and defended the near post. But instead, on this occasion, they all came inside the six-yard box and I was suddenly out of position. The cross came towards the centre-back who was against me and boom: goal! We were 1-0 down. Can you imagine what my head was like? We could be losing the title because of me! They were celebrating and I was walking back to my position. Then I saw Sergio Agüero. His face! He was like, 'Give the ball to me. Give it to me!' His eyes were ablaze: 'I will do it now!' they screamed. Fucking hell. A few minutes later, he had equalised. Then David Silva, the second. Then Aymeric Laporte, corner, the third. Half-time, 3-1. I've never seen such confidence in a player as I did that day in Sergio. I remember thinking, 'This is a fucking big player, huh? Give me this ball, I will do it now.' Wow! Mahrez scored the fourth, we won 4-1 and won the league. But this is the difference. When you have so much quality, you have this confidence. With the mentality of Sergio, no one can stop you. That's what I want to remember for the rest of my life.

The next weekend we had the FA Cup final against Watford. In the week running up to the game I got food poisoning and lost nearly four kilos. I could only drink water and couldn't eat anything. I think it was some sushi I had. And when you get food poisoning from seafood, it's the worst thing you can have. I swear, I thought I was going to die during the night. No joke! I woke up during the night, two days before the game. I went to the bathroom and really needed to get all of it out of my system. But there was no more food inside. And the spasms in my stomach were so bad. I was sweating. At some point, after a few minutes, I started to relax. I lay down and just slept on the bathroom tiles. I zoned out, knowing that in 48 hours the FA Cup final would come around.

The next day we travelled to London. I trained somehow, but that was scary because I was drained and had no food inside, no energy. For four days I just had water. By now, my normal weight was 72.5 kg, but I was 69 kg. And, no, I didn't tell anyone. It was the last game of the season. I really wanted to play. You know, it's the FA Cup final at Wembley! That's how I prepared for my first ever FA Cup final. It was one of the toughest games for me physically, but I played 90 minutes and fortunately we won 6-0 to complete a domestic treble, the first time an English team had achieved that. I was thankful it wasn't a close match.

Then, after we won the game and had gone to the dressing room, Vinny asked everyone to sit down in the corner. The Wembley dressing room is a circle, but he got everyone on one side. He takes the FA Cup, puts it on the table, places his arm on the cup, and says, 'Okay, guys, this was my last game for this club.' Oh my God, half the team were crying. Brian Kidd was crying. We had suspected it might be his last game, but this just made it final. And he gave such an amazing speech. It was a tough moment for everyone because Vincent was more than just a player for this club. He was absolutely the best captain I ever had in my life.

My first season had been incredible, winning a Premier League and Carabao Cup medal. But this season was off the scale. Now I had won the treble of Premier League, FA Cup and Carabao Cup, played in both cup finals and in 14 Premier League games. There was still a lot to learn, but I was feeling more and more that I belonged.

7

Cracking the Code of Football

Liverpool in the Community Shield at Wembley. The game could go either way. But we end up winning it on penalties. What stuck in my mind after, though, was the quality of my opponent on the day. With the greatest respect to my friend Riyad Mahrez – who had made my life very difficult in that match against Leicester City – Mohamed Salah is the toughest player I've ever played against.

Why Salah? He's just so dynamic and relentless. And in that game, Liverpool had worked out the perfect ploy to make my afternoon a nightmare. It was almost a set-piece for them, even though the ball was in play. The pattern was always the same. We're in a mid-block. Virgil van Dijk has the ball deep in his own half. He touches it onto his right foot, rolls it, and his body shape tells me he's getting ready to hit one of those long diagonal balls. That very second, Georginio Wijnaldum sprints between me and the left-sided centre-back, Nicolás Otamendi. My priority is always inside, so I move across to close the gap. But Salah moves wide and drops back a bit. Van Dijk's diagonal ball goes straight to his legs, soft like butter. Salah can receive the ball on the half turn and run. Because he's dropped back and I'm closer to goal, inside, there are about ten to 15 metres between him and me. For him, that's like a runway. Once he accelerates towards goal in that kind of space, he's essentially unstoppable. He's left-footed, so naturally likes to cut inside, but if you give him too much space trying to cover the shot, he can push past you on the right as well. And then you're gone. There were five moments like that that I just about survived.

At half-time, Pep was speaking about a few general things. But I needed an answer to this problem. I went up to Mikel and explained my predicament. 'What should I do? I need to close the inside lane. If I get too close to Salah, I can't deal with Wijnaldum's run.'

He said, 'Yes, of course, you need to close the inside. In this case, what you have to do is ask Raheem Sterling to drop and help you out. Tell him to forget about Trent Alexander-Arnold and come back. He has enough time to fill in while the ball travels. There's no other way.'

And that's what I did. There's no shame in asking some of your team-mates to help out against a player like that, otherwise you'll be lost. He's just so explosive and pacy. When you're up against him, you feel the danger on your skin. He's the worst. Because he's the best.

***

'Alex, come on!' sighed Pep.

It was March 2021. I was a bit more established in the team by now and we were training the day before flying out to play a Champions League match against Borussia Mönchengladbach. It was that typical pre-match training session where you are going through some patterns of play for the game, no opposition pressing, just a run-through. And everything was fine. I was doing well, training properly, passing cleanly when I hit, not a bad pass, but not the perfect pass, to the wrong foot of one of the players.

'Alex, come on!'

In my head, I was thinking: 'Come on? You don't say anything to anyone else when someone plays a bad pass! But when I play one bad pass during the session, you complain like this?'

That was in my head. And then out loud I said: 'Mister! Like, I just did one wrong pass, you know?'

And his reaction was incredible.

'Oh, okay, sorry, sorry, Mr Zinchenko. Sorry,' said Pep. 'Okay, guys, thank you, everyone, inside.'

And he went in, walked to the changing room. Training over, all because I talked back. I knew I was in trouble after this. In my head, I was like: 'Okay, now I'm benched tomorrow for sure. I shouldn't have said a word.' But sometimes when you don't play, you keep everything inside. You train well, you work hard, and then one wrong pass and they just scream your name, and you just blow up. But this is where you need to control yourself.

The Mönchengladbach game, I was on the bench. No surprise there. But I played in the next Premier League match against West Ham. After the game, I bumped into Pep in the corridor, and said: 'Boss, I apologise for my behaviour. It was not right, for sure. It wasn't a great pass. And I promise you it's not going to happen again.'

He replied, 'Alex, it's fine. There's no problem. It's a working moment. We shake hands, we move on, you know.'

But this was significant to me. First of all, I was so young. Second, let's be honest, in terms of these players around me, how can I be the one to complain? The others work hard, and who am I to talk back, being in probably one of the best teams in the world? I still really regret it, but it was a good lesson for me. Because life is so tough at Manchester City. Imagine, there are 24 world-class players in the squad, and you start as number 25, not a guaranteed squad member on match days, let alone a guaranteed starter. You are constantly looking over your shoulder. You're never quite sure if you enjoy the full confidence of your coach and that of your team-mates who are, to a fault, all world-class. People don't realise how hard it is to be playing under a cloud.

Anatoliy became like another father to me in those days. You cannot imagine how many times he convinced me to stay at City rather than leave the club because I wasn't first choice, or even second. The times when I didn't play, what kept me there and motivated was that I knew this experience would help me, that I was learning and going to become a much better footballer with these people around me. Not just the players, but the coaching staff and Pep. And I always said to myself: 'When my opportunity comes, I'm going to seize it.' I had to keep that in my head to motivate myself every single day. Because I'm telling you, when you work so hard, train so hard, when it looks like you really deserve to play and then you see your team-mate, who is playing the same position, get injured and then Pep plays a centre-back in your position, it kills you! That's the worst feeling in football. I felt it a lot during those periods.

Usually when players don't play, it's 'I want to go! I need to play!' And some of my team-mates, big names, used to tell me, 'Alex, you need to play. How old are you? Nineteen? Twenty? You need to play. Go somewhere else!' When everyone was pushing me, only Anatoliy said: 'Stay there. Stay where you are. Trust me. Trust the process.' I never told him that I lacked belief at times. He must have sensed it. 'You will be part of this team,' he said. 'You will be there. This is your place.' Every day when I got back after training, he drilled that message into me. We don't speak that often any more, Anatoliy and I. Everyone's very busy with their lives. Maybe he thinks I forgot about those things. But I didn't, and I never will. I will always be grateful to him for the support he gave me during those days of perpetual self-doubt.

I knew I had to improve my game in all aspects to have any hope of being part of this team. Most of the time, there was one or even two players ahead of me, but I took some comfort from the fact that Pep still kept me on. I thought to myself, if he didn't believe in me at all, I would have long been shown the door or sent down to the Under-21s. But I was always with the first team. That must mean something.

What also helped me deal with never feeling secure in my position at City was my love for football. Just being able to share the pitch with those guys was never less than a wonder. I drove to training every day looking forward to playing at this level. Even as a seasoned professional, I still can't walk past a football without kicking it. Sometimes I joined in the odd training session with a City youth team, to spy on the next generation coming through and give them a bit of a boost. I knew how much it would have meant to me if one of the senior players had played with us when I was in their place. One time, while I was running through a park in Manchester, I saw these kids pinging balls to each other and, again, I couldn't help myself and got in on the action.

Even in situations where Pep has to try to keep 25 players on board, he somehow finds a way to make you feel special. One moment I will remember for the rest of my life was before a Manchester United game. Everyone was fit, absolutely everyone. On the matchday-minus-one training session, he mixed up the teams. You couldn't tell the starting line-up. And he called us into a circle on the pitch after the training and said: 'Guys, you are fucking unbelievable. All of you. You've trained absolutely amazing. Help me, please. Help me to choose my XI for tomorrow.

I don't know who to choose for tomorrow. I can't do it. You are all so good. Absolutely amazing. All of you, you deserve to play. Fernandinho, you are the captain. You pick the team. This is the toughest thing for me in this job, so just do it.'

And Fernandinho replied: 'No, no, no, boss! This is your job. This is what you are getting money for!' Pep was trying to send a message to the team. Of course we weren't going to choose the starting XI there. But it was Pep's way of communicating to us that we were all special, even those who didn't play.

Another game against United, away this time, was a similar experience. Normally Pep gives the starting XI at the team meeting before we travel to the ground or go to the dressing room. But that time, he didn't say what the team was at the meeting. When the meeting was over, we went to the bus, and as we were driving to the ground no one knew who was going to play. I've never seen this in my life. We came to the dressing room, the small away dressing room in Old Trafford, and he said, 'Guys, all of you do your activation, get some treatment and be ready to play. I will give you a line-up in 20 minutes.' He told us the starting XI for the derby just before we went out to warm up. Can you imagine this?

Pep, as everybody knows, is meticulous about patterns of passing and the shape of the team, but he trusts his players to motivate themselves and others. If someone wanted to say something before a game in the dressing room, he encouraged it. Away to Real Madrid in the

Champions League, in the round of 16 in 2019-20, İlkay got everyone into the huddle. He wasn't captain at the time and usually one of the quieter characters, but he had obviously thought deeply about what needed to be done to survive the hostile atmosphere of the Santiago Bernabéu, as he had played there twice with Borussia Dortmund a few years earlier. 'Okay guys, listen,' he started. 'First 20 minutes, we just stay in focus. We don't concede the ball. Trust me. With the help of the crowd, they will attack and try to hurt us in the first 15, 20 minutes. If we get through that, we will win the game, because we have an amazing team. We will create a lot of chances. Just stay focused, every single second. Against this team, in this stadium, that's key.'

It was an amazing speech, very to the point. I remember I looked over to Pep and he looked so pleased. For a manager, it must be wonderful to see players taking responsibility and coaching themselves. But it doesn't happen by chance. First, you need to ensure you have the right characters in the dressing room, players with talent and personality. Second, you need to empower them. There are managers who only want to hear themselves speak. They want to decide everything, control everything, manage everything. Pep is not like that at all. You could see how proud he was that İlkay spoke that night. That showed him that he was doing a great job, that his team were on a path to greatness, especially since the boys went on to play a stupendous match that night, following İlkay's advice. We won 2-1.

CRACKING THE CODE OF FOOTBALL

Gundo wasn't the only one to speak up. A few players addressed the team before games, and each time everyone listened attentively and with great respect. In those moments, you feel a bond that's stronger than being teammates. You are like family. And when you go onto the pitch in that kind of mood, playing like one big family, it's very hard to get beat.

What a place to be. I was saying to my wife after I left City how lucky I was to have worked with probably the best manager in football history. It's impossible to buy this experience. You can read a thousand books but being there, on the inside, and seeing every meeting, to be immersed in it, is priceless. I've seen some players perhaps a bit sleepy in meetings because, honestly, if you are not fully focused, you can switch off in any meeting with any manager. With Pep, you really have to concentrate. If you don't understand what he wants, his ideas, you're going to suffer. You won't be able to function properly.

I've seen some players asleep in his meetings because, when your brain is overloaded, you just give up and shut your eyes. I've seen some players actually do that. But for me, it was like a course in higher football. I always sat next to İlkay. We were very similar in that we both really wanted to learn. Obviously, İlkay is much smarter and more experienced than me, because he had already played at the highest level. But even he was learning, watching and listening to all Pep's meetings and really enjoying them. Not all players are like that. But I was like a sponge, soaking everything up. I used to write down notes about all the training exercises in a big folder and often discussed Pep's ideas with Vlada, who loves football and used to play herself. I stopped doing that, which is probably something I regret a bit. My uncle and friends used to tell me, 'Take notes, take notes!' I thought everything would stay in my head forever, but I wish now that I had written more of it down.

You know why Pep's teams win so often? It's because he's cracked the code of football. His is a simple formula, when you think about it, a system that gets you into dangerous areas with astonishing regularity and tilts the scales inevitably in your favour. He has found a way to control a game that is essentially uncontrollable. His teams score more goals and concede fewer goals because they control games more.

It goes something like this.

To start with, you have to have possession. As long as you have the ball, the opposition can't score. More importantly, having the ball allows you to control the rhythm of the game as well as the space it's being played in. By moving the ball, you move the opposition, because they have to react. If you move it well enough, you will create gaps in their defence that you can exploit. The foundation of this possession game is pressing, the attempt to win the ball back as quickly as possible when they have it. Growing up, I had managers tell me you can only press high up the pitch for 20, 30 minutes. After that, you will get tired. No. At City, you press for 90 minutes.

In possession, your initial aim is to play through the first line of pressing. That's if they're courageous enough to be pressing at all, as opposed to barricading themselves deep in their own half. From the goal kicks onwards, everything was carefully planned, though the exact way we played depended on the opponent. Do they press with one striker? Do they press with two players? Is one of the centre-midfielders 'jumping' to press one of our centre-backs?

Pep gives you a plan to bypass the press, a road map. You do it by creating a numerical advantage and more passing options than the opposition can cut off. Maybe the full-back would drop into midfield. Maybe he will be pushed out wide. One of the midfielders might go low. This all needs to happen automatically, without thinking. 'As if you're brushing your teeth,' Pep would say. And you needed to be able to change the map yourself if the opposition changed their pressing during the game.

If their striker is a fast, ferocious type like Gabriel Jesus, who is probably one of the best in the world when it comes to harassing defenders, it's a nightmare for the centre-backs in the build-up. We found it much easier against Cristiano Ronaldo, for example. Don't get me wrong, everyone knows he's one of the greatest in this game. But defensively, he didn't pay a lot of attention. He was just focusing on having the ball, getting ready to make a big impact when he got it. Playing past that kind of centre-forward takes less planning.

To play out from the back with maximum versatility and control, you need to have technical centre-backs and a keeper who must be able to play like a midfielder, with his feet. If the opposition continue to press once the first wave is broken, you have a huge advantage up front: yours is one of the best strikers in the world and they are giving him space by continuing to attack the ball. Usually the striker will use this space to destroy you. When the opposition don't press and sit deeper, however, then everyone needs to respect their positions, which enables us to traverse midfield.

The trick is to manipulate the opposition so that your dangerous players end up in one-vs-one or two-vs-two situations, especially on the flanks. How do you do that against deep defences? You do it by dominating possession in the opposition half with players who can keep the ball under huge pressure, by pushing back the opposition further and further and then switching play. Take Jack Grealish. Pundits and other so-called experts often criticised him for not scoring enough goals or producing assists. They didn't understand his role. Jack is very good at keeping the ball while running at defenders. What he does for City is to push defensive lines further towards their own goal. That gives the rest of the team time to move closer and into position. He gets all the attention, luring two or three over to his side, then lays the ball off for a switch to the other side, where the opponent is exposed. Bingo.

Pep's mantra was: 'If we start our build-up on the left side, we need to finish our action on the right. Then their team are getting pulled out of shape, they move towards the ball and forget the guy on the other end while we respect our positions and keep our structure. That's why we always need to have our extra pocket guy on the other side, behind our winger, so that the winger has this advantage against their full-back.' So for example, we would have the ball on the left with De Bruyne, he pings it across, and suddenly Sterling is running down the right against their full-back. This is the game, right there. This is where we used to kill a lot of teams. But it only works if you keep your position, especially the players in the pockets.

The wide spaces need to be occupied as well, and of course the striker plays an important role too. Its exact nature depends on how many players they have in the back line, whether there are five or four. Sometimes the striker can drop to make some advantages in the middle or to drag the opposition centre-back with him to create the space for the No. 10 or No. 8 to run in behind. With all that going on, Pep also warned his defenders to control the 'man up the pitch' and prepare for the counter-attacks. While we were in possession, we still needed to think about defending.

When I used to play on the left, the aim was to get David Silva and Leroy Sané either one vs one or two vs two against the defenders. If the opposition cannot defend in numbers, having been stretched by our approach play, they don't stand much chance against guys of that quality. Pep used to say, 'My job is to get you into the final third and into the best situation, one vs one. I'm not going to teach you how to dribble, how to cross the ball, how to finish the action once you're there. You're being paid big money, you're one of the best players in the world, you're playing for a big club like Man City. After that, it's about the talent God gave you. You have so much talent, use it!' As for me, a full-back, my task was to get Leroy Sané, Raheem Sterling, Riyad Mahrez or Jack Grealish the ball. Ten opportunities per game, one vs one with the full-back, how many times do you think they would get past them? At least seven times, no? And of those seven moves, at least four would result in high-probability scoring chances. You will have noticed how many tap-ins we scored. It's just simple mathematics.

I remember one game I played behind David Silva and Leroy. We struggled to create chances. I always used to be tucked in a little bit, Silva was in the pocket, or between the lines, and Leroy high wide. We couldn't get past the defensive line, so we decided to rotate. Silva dropped, Leroy came into the pocket, and I went high.

Pep hadn't instructed us to do that. It was our idea, born spontaneously on the pitch. Things still didn't work well, however. In the end, we somehow won the game. But the day after, the moment I got to the training ground, Vinny grabbed me. 'Zinna, come here.' He took a pen and showed me the positions we had occupied, and how I had ended up the higher player at times. Then he wrote down some numbers: 'Leroy Sané, 17 games, ten goals, five assists. David Silva, 15 games, four goals, ten assists. Zinchenko, ten games, one assist.' He said, 'Look, every time you go up front, our chances of scoring are smaller. That's why I was screaming at you throughout the game

Orthodox Christmas celebrations in January 1999 when I was just two years old.

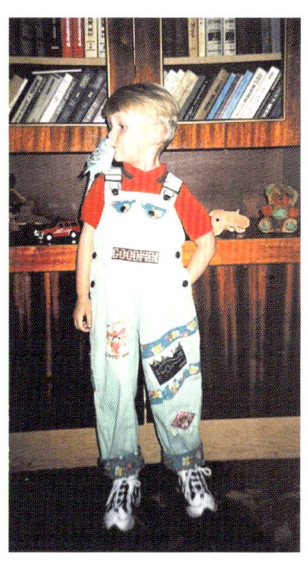

With my pet budgerigar.

An early football medal, while David Beckham watches on.

All dressed up for the school photo (I'm fourth from the left, in the top row).

Challenging Héctor Bellerín in the Youth Champions League game between Arsenal and Shakhtar Donetsk in February 2014. We lost 3-1, but I later learned that my efforts had been noticed.

Scoring my first international goal, in a friendly against Romania before Euro 2016 – not only was I the youngest to score for Ukraine, I did it with a broken toe.

I'd first met Vlada via social media when I was 14, but it wasn't until the Poland game in Euro 2016 that we finally met in person and I was able to give her my shirt.

A rare appearance during my disappointing loan spell at PSV Eindhoven in 2016–17, but it was a period when I learned resilience.

I made a late substitute appearance against Bayern Munich at the Allianz Arena – it was my Champions League debut, but we were well beaten.

Some advice from PSV manager Phillip Cocu. I got the strong impression that he hadn't much wanted me to sign for the club, but even so, it is always up to the player to show what he can offer.

My first official game for Manchester City, against Wolves in the Carabao Cup in October 2017, as Gabriel Jesus and I double up on Ben Marshall. Pep Guardiola had promised that I would get some minutes that season, but I played too cautiously that day.

Enjoying my first Premier League title win in 2018 with my mum, Iryna, and stepdad, Viktor.

After being left out of the away leg against my old club Shakhtar Donetsk, I was desperate to play against them when they came to Manchester in the Champions League in November 2018.

Pep Guardiola always seemed to know what to say to inspire me. Here he congratulates me after I'd scored the winning penalty in the Carabao Cup shoot-out against Leicester City in December 2018.

A head-in-hands moment after my mistake enables Southampton to take a 1-0 lead in our Premier League game in December 2018. When Pep made an example of me at half-time, it wasn't in the way I'd expected.

Celebrating Carabao Cup success with Vincent Kompany, who was such a formidable leader and inspiration in the City squad; his intensity was unmatched.

Anatoliy Patuk and I celebrate after City completed a unique clean sweep of domestic trophies in 2018–19.

Mo Salah is one of the toughest opponents I've ever faced, and in the 2019 Community Shield Liverpool perfected a tactic that left me chasing him all over the pitch.

After I'd fumbled my planned marriage proposal to Vlada on the day Ukraine qualified for Euro 2020, I filled the Olympic stadium with thousands of roses for the official photograph of our engagement.

Celebrating not just my goal in a friendly against Cyprus in 2021, but also the imminent arrival of our baby Eva.

After a poor run in the group stages of Euro 2020, we had all come under a great deal of criticism for our efforts, so when I scored our first goal against Sweden in the Round of 16, it was a vital moment in the match.

Less than a week after Russia invaded Ukraine, I was offered the captain's armband as City took on Peterborough in the FA Cup. The support for my country from everyone meant so much to me.

We didn't make it easy for ourselves, but in my last match for City we secured the Premier League title with a great comeback win against Aston Villa. At the end, I placed the Ukraine flag around the trophy.

Vlada and Eva join me to pose with the trophy that marked the end of six years as a City player.

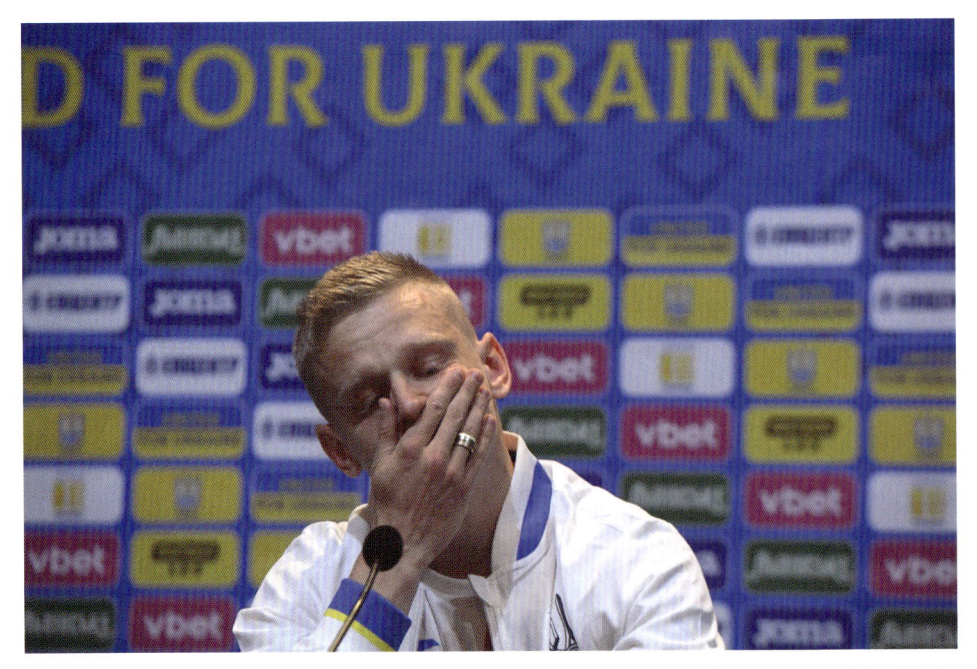

I found it hard to contain the emotion of what we were trying to achieve ahead of the World Cup play-off against Scotland; this wasn't just a football match but an opportunity to show everyone what Ukraine means to us.

When we lined up to sing the national anthem ahead of our World Cup play-off, the support from everyone in the stadium made Scotland's Kieran Tierney say 'I thought we were playing away!'

Posing for the cameras as I sign for Arsenal in July 2022. After City, there was no other club or manager in the Premier League that I would have joined than Mikel Arteta's Arsenal.

Beating our north London rivals Spurs 2-0 at their ground in January 2023 gave the whole squad real belief we could sustain our title challenge that season.

When I ran over to the fans after our stoppage-time winner against Manchester United later that month, I almost regretted it, as the noise was so loud I thought my ears might fall off.

Celebrating with Mikel Arteta after another late comeback, this time against Bournemouth, earned us all three points. The manager's brilliance had brought a new belief to the side and to the fans.

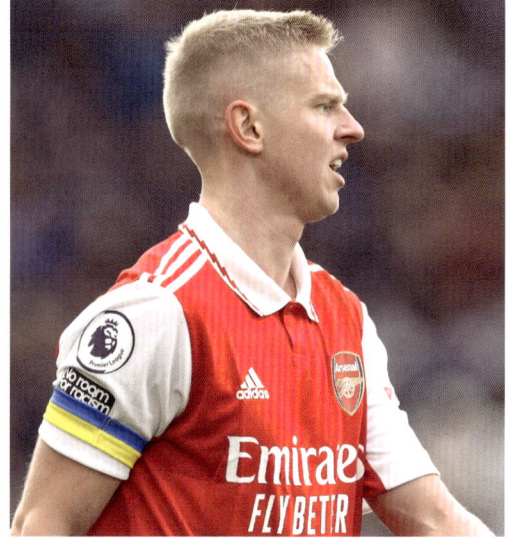

One year on from the invasion of my country by Russia, the team asked if I could captain Arsenal for the day, as we took on Leicester City. It's so important to me that we continue to remind the world of what is happening in Ukraine.

With Andriy Shevchenko outside the Mykhailo Kotsyubinsky Lyceum in the Chernihiv region, which had been destroyed by the Russians, and the United24 charity was helping to rebuild.

After nine months of work, the Game4Ukraine finally went ahead at Stamford Bridge in August 2023, and a crowd of 30,000 came along to support the cause. Here, Arsène Wenger, who had spotted me playing for Shakhtar almost a decade earlier, and I embrace.

Congratulating Kai Havertz after his goal against Brentford in November 2023. He'd come under a lot of media criticism since his arrival, but in the squad we knew just how much he brought to the team.

Our dogs, Louie (wearing the medal) and Mia.

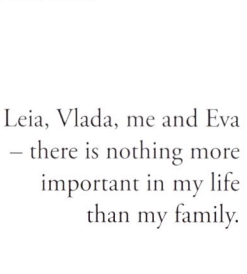

Leia, Vlada, me and Eva – there is nothing more important in my life than my family.

Artem Dovbyk and I celebrate after beating Iceland to qualify for the finals of Euro 2024, ensuring we could help keep Ukraine in everyone's minds.

After our poor performance in the first game of Euro 2024, we were so much better against Slovakia, competing for everything to win 2-1 – but we couldn't get out of the group stage.

For Ukraine.

to stay where you were. Let them go up. They have amazing numbers and they can create more than you in that spot.' I couldn't argue with that. Football is about maximising your chances of success in a game of random events. We weren't doing that.

Pep saw everything. As I said, he would get upset in training when someone played a pass into the wrong foot of a team-mate. You might think what's the difference, but if the player receiving the pass has to turn or control the ball with an extra touch instead of collecting it in his stride, it's a split second lost, a breather for the opposition that will help them get back into shape. With newcomers to the team, he spent quite of bit of time teaching them about the right body orientation, how you need to position yourself in relation to the ball and your opponents, how you moved to open up the pass.

Most of the time we played against teams in a low block: in other words, teams that defended deep. He absolutely hated it when one of our defenders had the ball with ten or 15 metres of space ahead of them but simply passed it sideways. He used to say: 'Unless you break the line of defence with a pass, there's no point playing it. If you have space ahead of you, run forward with the ball. Then someone will be drawn out from the block to attack you and you can find a team-mate in the space that's opened up.' That idea was very relevant for my game. If there was no incisive pass on, he wanted me to drive on to attract a marker and then play it to the winger, who could then go man vs man.

So it's kind of the opposite of what some people think about Pep's football. They believe he loves tiki-taka, passing for passing's sake, that it's some kind of fetish for him. But Pep abhors sterile possession: passing has to always be meaningful to him.

Mentally, it's a tough regime at City. Physically as well, when we played every three days. Pep used to say to us all the time: 'Guys, trust me, you are not tired here,' pointing to his legs. 'It's here,' he said, pointing to his head. 'Trust me, I know what I'm talking about. You are not tired. Your legs are fine. It has to be like this. You are going to play every three days.' And I think he's right. We underestimate our brain. We only know a tiny fraction of how our brain works. The brain is our main strength. The rest is just the connection between muscles and brain.

Pep's principles are non-negotiable. 'From the keeper to the striker, we have to put the ball on the grass, make 1,000 passes and pick the right moment,' he once said. But the tactics can change depending on the game. I remember when we played against Liverpool away, at Anfield in February 2021. It was Covid time, no fans. On match day minus one, in training there were two groups: one group worked with him on tactics and the other did some positional game, set pieces, crosses, shooting and finishing. The group on tactics with Pep had players in each position, building up, but without any opposition. So everyone stayed in their position and just moved the ball, but he said: 'Guys, let's start from the goal kick, everyone in position, just visualise where they are. But I want you to make at least three or four touches on the ball.' So we start with the keeper, he passed the ball to the centre-back, he does three, four touches, passes the ball, another player does three, four touches, passes the ball.

'Do you know why we are taking extra touches?' Pep asked. 'I tell you. Most of the teams come to Anfield and shit themselves. They want to play one-touch, two-touch. "Oh, don't give me the ball! Oh you take it!" But you have to play with big balls at Anfield! Big balls! "Give me the ball!" Demand it! If you need to dribble past two or three players, do it. But play football. I want you to play football.' And he did this speech again on the pitch on the day. 'I want you to make as many touches as you want in this game, because teams coming here are scared. They play one or two touches, and that's what Liverpool like, because they get the ball back so quickly, and they just do their electric counter-attacks with Mané, Salah, Firmino. I want you to keep the ball. Be brave. Play your football!' And we were doing this from the start of the game and we won 4-1. We destroyed them. You think, 'This guy is so crazy!' But he's right. You have to enjoy it at Anfield, play your game. If not, they're going to eat you.

One example of the detail Pep goes into? When we had meetings, he would always stop on a clip and point out the actions of the opposition manager on the touchline, saying, 'Guys, look at their manager. Look at what he's asking his player to do in this action. He's showing him to play the ball in that channel. So that's what they will try to do most of the time. That's what the manager is asking them to do during the game. So we need to be mentally ready for it. Maybe take a few extra steps back, to be first on the ball while they're playing that channel.' He pays a lot of attention not just to the players but also the manager. I've never seen this before.

But it's so demanding, playing for Pep. Everything looks so neat, and the football seems like it is free-flowing. But it's difficult because you are not at liberty to do whatever you like; it's definitely not a free role. You are playing a symphony as an orchestra, not jazz in a smoky cellar. Each action, you need to know what to do, that you have to move like this or pass like that. And it must be like this, not any other action. City is like a machine. You cannot be anywhere you want. You just need to be where you have been coached to be. You're a small cog.

Sometimes you can feel a little bit like a robot. Don't get me wrong, it was sheer pleasure being there. But before, at FC Ufa, apart from some basic instructions, you would have freedom to think for yourself. The game was smaller then. You had one or two basic jobs and, beyond that, you could improvise a bit and go where the game took you, to an extent. At City, you always need to think about the bigger picture, about your positioning in relation to the ball, your team-mates and your opponents. You have to hit those precise coordinates while everything is moving at 100 miles per hour, otherwise the whole thing can fall apart. You are part of a mechanism, a number in a giant equation designed by a genius to produce a reliable outcome, even though there are hundreds of variables. You cannot switch off at any point. Mentally, that's quite a challenge. Sometimes people would think, 'Oh, it must be so easy to be all around all those great players. Anyone could probably play there and look half decent, surrounded by all those super players.' But trust me, it's not like that.

And the running! It was incredible how much we ran. Pep would say, 'Guys, do you know why my Barcelona team was so successful? Because we used to run like animals.' But with Pep's training you can run for kilometres and not even notice it, because you're enjoying it. There would be sessions where you're on the ball, doing some football but also running. And when you look back you realise there wasn't much football, more running. But because of the football, you don't notice how much you have run and you enjoy it.

A lot of the game is won or lost in the mind. At one Premier League away game in the midst of winter, it was freezing cold and raining non-stop. Pep called everyone in after warm-up. He said, 'Guys, today, you decide how you're going to play.' He rolled up his sleeves. 'Like this?' Then he stretched his sleeves to hide his fingers. 'Or like this?' That's all we needed that day. We went out and won big. It's such a small, simple thing to say, but if it's said in the right moment, the impact is huge. Pep's timing for these small interventions was always spot-on.

8

Porto Blues

The 2019-20 season was interrupted by Covid. We won the Carabao Cup again and I played in the final, 2-1 vs Aston Villa. But that was one of the last games before the season stopped because of Covid restrictions. By then we had already messed up the league. Liverpool were superb that season and dropped only two points until the end of February, so we had already lost touch by the time the Covid break came.

It was a crazy time. All of us were in shock. Football just stopped. My family were in Ukraine at that moment, and I was alone with my dogs in the apartment in Manchester. And we couldn't even go out for training. We had to stay at home. None of us knew when the games would restart. As a professional footballer, you are used to having every moment of the season more or less mapped out for you, but there we were, basically waking up to a void every day. How can you prepare yourself like that?

We were doing online courses on bikes and some other exercises for the core and so on, but it wasn't enough for me. When you train on the pitch, you burn many more calories than when you're out in the woods running alone, because you cannot push yourself as much. When you play football and compete with each other, there's a completely different intensity. But you don't even feel or see it. You cannot replicate that by yourself, without the ball.

Some players dealt with it much better than me. I guess it comes down to the way your metabolism works. City did a DEXA scan of all the players when we were allowed to train together again. I think I broke all the records in terms of body fat. I was one of the fattest guys in the team; my face was a circle. I had never been this badly out of shape. Even to this day, Riyad and I joke about it, because we're so close. Those were the only three days in his life when he destroyed me in the training session, because I wasn't ready yet. I was nearly crying.

I don't think it was all my fault; my body just reacted very badly to inactivity. Raheem, for example, came back perfect. He said, 'Guys, when we're doing online training sessions, I switched off my camera, played PlayStation and drank a can of Fanta.' I'm not sure it's true, because he certainly didn't look it. He came back fit and I came back fat. I blame my bad genes. Luckily, I can at least sleep well after late matches. You still have so much adrenaline in your body, and your legs are aching quite badly. A lot of players struggle with shutting down. They take sleeping pills to take the edge off. I've played cards – Uno – in the hotel with guys who have popped a pill and are ready to go to bed. They get so drowsy, it's a bit of an unfair advantage. And I'm not sure it doesn't affect you in the long run, if it becomes a habit.

Others might get away with the odd indiscretion, but I have to be on top of it all the time and really look after myself, eating well, sleeping well, doing extra physio sessions. I can't take the punishment some players do to themselves. I have seen guys who can have a few drinks all week or consume chocolate before games and still eat up their opponents on the pitch. They're so big and powerful that nothing affects them. Even if I live like a monk, I still can't get near them, as far as the physicality goes.

I was playing more though, making 19 Premier League appearances that season. I felt I was growing as a man and as a football player. Dealing with the pressure that comes from not being one of the important players in the squad and the rumours about being sold every six months was getting a little easier for me. Or perhaps I should say, I learned how to handle it better. I was able block out those fears and insecurities by focusing on the many positives. Every day, I reminded myself that I had won the football lottery. I was playing with the best players in the world and getting coached by the best manager.

Before Covid, we had beaten Real Madrid in the first leg of the Champions League last 16. But it was strange. The first leg was played in February and then there was this huge break. Because everyone focused on completing the domestic leagues first, the Champions League didn't resume again until August, which is when we played the second leg. We won that and qualified for the hastily arranged eight-team tournament in Portugal, which was designed to get the Champions League finished in a week. We lost 3-1 to Lyon in our quarter-final game in Lisbon, a huge shock which had everyone devastated. Of course, the critics were delighted. They kept bringing up that City and Pep couldn't win the Champions League. We had lost to Monaco, Liverpool, Tottenham, all in pretty unlucky circumstances.

We didn't play well against Lyon, but there was another big element of misfortune then, too. Since the format had been changed to single knockout ties, we had no chance to react to the defeat. I'm 100 per cent certain that we would have gone through playing them twice. Pep would have analysed our mistakes and set us up perfectly for the return leg.

There was a lot of pressure on the club to win the Champions League. You could feel it inside the dressing room, but Pep was unfazed. He hated losing big games as much as anyone, of course, but he never lost his temper. What all the haters and the pundits talking nonsense didn't see was that Pep always kept calm, was very patient with us and never changed his approach, come what may.

After big defeats, he would focus on the positives. 'I can't fault your desire to win today, guys,' he used to say. 'You created three times as many chances as them but didn't score. Don't beat yourselves up about it. Don't get your heads down. Be together, stick together, put your phones away and talk to each other. Talk about why it happened, what we should do, what can be done better.' That was very good counselling. Today, there's a tendency for players to all pick up their phones to check on social media or speak to their families the minute the game is over. But you have to use those moments together in the dressing room to connect with each other and share ideas, especially after defeats.

The next season, 2020-21, was better and we were almost back to our best, despite playing most of the season in empty stadiums due to Covid. It was weird, playing in silence, but we adjusted well. We won the Carabao Cup again, although this time I was on the bench once more. Why? Because I didn't deserve to be the in the starting line-up. Simple as. My first reaction was to be angry and frustrated, but with Pep, you always realised after a while that he was taking decisions for the right reasons and on merit. Personal feelings, favouritism or dislike just don't come into it for him. He used to say, 'I'm not handing out any presents here. If you play, that means you deserve to play.' And it was true.

That attitude is one of the things I liked most about him. He's obviously a genius tactically; we don't need to mention that. But he also has this knack of picking the right team, looking carefully at everyone's form, and then at the players and qualities he needs for the specific game plan.

In any case, I was often involved, playing 32 games that season, with 20 appearances in the Premier League as we won back our title. But the main focus was probably on the

Champions League, where we reached the final by beating Paris Saint-Germain in the semi. There were still some Covid restrictions when we went to Porto to play Chelsea in the final, meaning the attendance was limited. But we all appreciated this was a chance to silence Pep's critics.

We ought to have felt confident, because we had finished 19 points above Chelsea in the Premier League. But they had beaten us in the FA Cup semi-final in April and at the Etihad in the Premier League in May. Pep left Rodri out of the starting line-up, which was a surprise. But I wouldn't say it caused too many ripples in the dressing room. You are playing in a final. You are too preoccupied with yourself to worry about this or that player not playing. Secondly, even the best managers in the world make decisions that not everyone understands straight away. It's always been like that and will always be like that. In time, you might comprehend the rationale behind them, but either way, I would never complain. It's his job to make these calls, and he's incredibly good at it.

I still blame myself for the defeat, though. No two ways about it: I was shit. We didn't play well collectively, sure, but the goal that decided the game came from my man in that moment, Kai Havertz. Just before Mason Mount played him in, I didn't make the right move. Just a few steps would have been enough. But because I didn't, Havertz had half a metre on me. I'm just looking, chasing him, but he's running away and one-on-one with the keeper. Obviously, I was too slow to react at some point.

That was probably the worst day in my football life. A team like Chelsea, who had reached the Champions League final, are going to punish you for that. I watched the clip a few months later. I definitely didn't go looking for it. I was trying to just forget this – I stumbled across it somewhere on Instagram.

At half-time Pep was fuming, but not so much with me. I had never seen him like this before and never saw him this upset after, either. He mentioned the goal only briefly. But he was so angry, especially with the forward players because he said they were not hungry enough to create moments. He was saying, 'I don't recognise you. Guys, come on! It's the Champions League final!'

After the final whistle, it was an incredibly bad feeling. We went back to the hotel, where my wife was with our families. Vlada was waiting for me in the room. I just opened the door. We didn't say a word to each other. We just hugged. And both of us were crying. Honestly, she loves football more than me. A former player herself, she is obsessed with the game. We didn't even speak or sleep much. It was a terrible night. But then I received a call from Andriy Shevchenko. That was a huge lift for me. He said: 'Listen, you played amazing. Trust me. And it's not just my opinion.' He was trying to console me, because he knows from experience – Istanbul 2005 – how tough it is to lose a final. As Ukraine head coach, he also wanted to make sure I arrived with a more positive mindset at the Euros. He wanted to give me a confidence boost before the competition.

It worked. The Euros saved my life. I don't know how I would have reacted if I hadn't joined the national team straight after this final and kept chewing the defeat over for a few more weeks. The aftermath of the final had been crazy. I didn't sleep properly for three days. And I'm not sure how many times I ate. But the national team gave me a fresh outlook and a new goal to focus on. Win or lose, it was still an amazing experience to have played in the Champions League final. And even though it left me emotionally bruised, these things only make you stronger in the end.

I had another reason to keep things in perspective going forward, but only Vlada and I knew about it at the time. My plan was to tell the whole world during the friendly against Cyprus in Kharkiv, our last game before going to play in the group stage. For once, one of my plans worked. I scored a penalty to make it 2-0 just before half-time, put the ball under my shirt and my thumb into my mouth: the international goal celebration routine for having a baby. Vlada was seven months pregnant with Eva, our first daughter.

I was flush with happiness. It was such a beautiful day for everyone. I was about to become a dad and we had won 4-0. We were clapped off the pitch. After difficult months during Covid and lockdown, the country was looking forward to more normality and a successful competition. Everyone seemed proud of the national team. Looking back, it almost feels like the last moment of pure joy we experienced as a nation before results turned sour and a much more serious catastrophe struck.

Truth be told, we weren't very good at the Euros. You might say we were pretty awful. We lost 3-2 against the Netherlands, beat North Macedonia 2-1 and squeezed through as one of the fourth best third-placed teams after losing 1-0 to Austria. Personally, I was rubbish. But you can't feel sorry for yourself. What I have learned time and time again in my career is that dealing with pressure – whether it's being applied from the outside or a product of your own dashed hopes and frustrations – is one of the key skills necessary to have a successful career.

The whole of Ukraine seemed unhappy with us after the group stage. I was the target of a lot of criticism, because I played for City and had a higher profile than most. It was a similar story with Ruslan Malinovskyi. He had registered the most assists in Serie A that season with Atalanta. Back home, they expected so much more of us. Ruslan and I were put up for the press conference. It wasn't a pleasant experience. 'Why aren't you playing better?' You don't really have the answer, beyond stating the obvious, that your club form cannot always easily transfer to international football. But nobody wants to hear that.

Some people went way beyond legitimate criticism, however. One guy was mouthing off on television, telling everyone he had uncovered information that I had paid $1,000 per minute to Fomenko at Euro 2016, because I had needed those minutes to qualify for a work permit for the Premier League. No evidence provided, of course, just a bullshit story to get engagement and make a name for himself. I don't think many people believed such rubbish, but I would have preferred to do without this crap before a last-16 game against Sweden, who had topped their group ahead of Spain. I felt the weight of 50 kilos on my shoulders in the stadium tunnel before the match. The pressure was as bad as before the Champions League final.

We really pushed each other as a team in the days leading up to the game at Hampden Park, because the chance to flip the script was so great. We understood one thing: a win would turn everything around. Everyone would immediately forget our disastrous group stage and get excited by us reaching the first quarter-final at a Euros instead. From hate to love is only one step. That was our story.

We beat them 2-1 in extra time. Playing as a wing-back, I scored the opener – a crisp half-volley with the outside of my boot – and put in the cross for substitute Artem Dovbyk's winning header, too. I dedicated my man of the match trophy from UEFA to team-mate Artem Besedin, who had been hurt by a horror tackle that saw a Swedish player sent off and poor Artem miss a year of football with a smashed-up knee.

Getting into the quarter-finals of the Euros for the first time did change the mood of the nation, as predicted. Government ministers turned up in football shirts to a cabinet meeting, and the same people who slammed us for playing poorly in the group stage were now predicting we'd go all the way to the final at Wembley. But first, we had England to contend with, in Rome. Before the game, we huddled together and told each other: 'Guys, it's very important not to concede in the first 15, 20 minutes. If we can withstand that early pressure, we'll be there.' We went 1-0 down after four minutes. I hadn't even touched the ball yet. Not a great start. England scored three more goals, all from headers. It's okay to lose, but not 4-0. Losing 4-0 is a lot in a quarter-final. We were back down to earth with a big bump.

Sometimes I think that we lack the culture of winning in the national team. We are still a young country with limited experience at this level, but we should look to Croatia as an example. They've had an amazing run and approach every competition with real confidence. Looking at the bigger picture, it's obvious that they're doing a lot of things right in terms of organisation and their academies. They're a smaller country than us but produce so many talented players. We should learn from them.

9

Into the Darkness

When I came back to Man City at the start of the 2021-22 season, that mistake from the final in Porto still lived with me. It was a big emotional scar. I would find myself thinking: 'What if I had closed the gap and anticipated that run of Havertz?' And Fernandinho would remind me every day in training! He would point to his arm, where he was planning to get a tattoo of the Champions League trophy and say, 'Thanks Alex. No tattoo. Because of you!' He was only winding me up. I love this black humour. Because if you can't laugh at yourself, then you can't laugh with anyone. It helps to put the mistake in the past. But it took time. The pain was lodged very deeply inside, and it affected my performances. I kept telling myself, 'So you're playing badly because of the Champions League final three months earlier? Stop making excuses for yourself. Get a grip, man!' But it was true, that defeat was still chewing away at me, until I finally came to terms with it and moved on. I wish I could have been like Fernandinho and reacted differently; I would have performed so much better. Another huge lesson learned.

What would turn out to be my final season at City was yet another epic battle with Liverpool. This, along with 2018-19, was probably two of the best teams in the world at their absolute peak, winning game after game. The mentality of the team was: a draw is death. On the rare occasions we didn't win, I knew driving to the training ground the next day that everyone would feel absolutely disgusted with themselves. It's undoubtedly true that we pushed each other to the greatest heights. But on both occasions, when it was head-to-head until the very end, we came out on top.

I have often wondered how we were conditioned to peak just when it mattered, at the end of the season. Every single year, we got better and better after Christmas. I'm still not sure how – if I was, I'd sell that secret for lots of money – but looking back, I believe there were probably two reasons. One, the fitness coaches worked incredibly hard, combining the numbers from the GPS vests we all wore with information from the players. After every session, they asked us, 'How are the legs? How do you feel? How is your body after yesterday's match? Is it okay?' They asked the slightly older and experienced guys, never the youngsters, because the young ones don't feel it yet. I could play without a warm-up when I was 18. Then they would adjust the training session according to the answers and perhaps do a little less or a little more. It's obviously not an exact science and can be subjective, but players tend to be in tune with their bodies. By taking our views into account, they came upon a regime more refined than one that simply looked at the numbers.

But I found perhaps another explanation. You see, pre-season was often really difficult due to the many commercial trips the club made. Once, we were in Japan, and had three flights in 12 days. If you add the waiting in queues, the bus rides, the sponsorship meetings and the media duties, we spent as many days on the road as on the ground training. You can have the best fitness regime and really well-devised exercises with and without the ball, but it's still impossible to build up your physical condition properly that way. You simply don't have the time. Playing friendlies is no substitute. I understand why these trips are important for the clubs, but for the players it's not ideal, to say the least. Physically, I was dead at the end of every Community Shield game, because my body was never ready in mid-August. For five seasons, it was always the same. But once you're back in the regular rhythm, you can build and build, and by that time it's Christmas. That's why it wasn't so much a case of ending strongly but starting slowly for us. Heaven knows how well we would have done as a team if we had been able to spend more time on the training ground in pre-seasons and started the campaign in a better state. Maybe we would have won every single game? I'm only half-joking.

There was still a huge focus on the Champions League for us. And I was starting to feel a bit more secure about my starting position. In February 2022, I was left on the bench for the Champions League last-16 game against Sporting Lisbon. When that happens, it's important to hear from Pep's staff. Maybe someone will grab you by the shoulder and say, 'Alex, trust me, you're doing everything right, just keep going.' It's so important to get that reassurance. In my five years there, that didn't happen very often though. And I was only once in Pep's office in all my time there. I never went to his office to ask, 'Why don't I play?' and all these things. But it did happen on this one occasion. I played 90 minutes in the 4-0 win over Norwich on the Saturday, but the day before the game in Lisbon, I learned I was dropped to the bench. He put John Stones for the first time as a right-back and João Cancelo on the left, so he put a centre-back as right-back and a right-back on the left side.

I knocked on his door to ask Pep, 'Mister, maybe I'm doing something wrong? Can you explain? You told me after the [Norwich] game that I played well, and I just really want to know if I'm doing something wrong?' He just said, 'Alex, trust me, it's just my decision. In this game, I just really want to see João in this position, to come inside, but you're doing everything right. Just keep working hard, and everything will be good.' That's it. That was the one proper talk in private we ever had. I know other players would sometimes knock on his door to ask why they're dropped, and this must be the toughest part of the game, the toughest conversations for him.

What pushed me to go to his office before Sporting was that I had just read an interview with Andriy Voronin about his period at Liverpool. He was recalling how he didn't feature at some point, and then he went to the manager, Rafa Benitez, and asked: 'Why am I not playing?' And Benitez said, 'Look, you are not even complaining, so I was thinking that you're okay with it.' This interview pushed me to do something I had never done in my life. Because in my head, I thought every manager is always going to pick the best players and won't be influenced by those who complain the most. But maybe it makes a small difference. With Pep, most of the time, the guys who really deserve to play, they played. If you were amazing in training sessions during the week and your attitude was good, then you got your chance. He was fair. Yet Voronin's interview struck a chord with me. Sometimes you have to stick up for yourself. But soon, not starting a Champions League felt like an irrelevance compared with what happened back home.

***

All through the winter of 2021-22, Russian troops amassed near the border with Ukraine. People at home were worried, but the consensus was that Putin was bluffing, just making threats. Ukraine is a huge country. Trying to conquer it was madness. Nobody made contingency plans. People essentially continued to live their lives as normal.

But then, on 24 February 2022, my wife woke me up by crying. She said, 'It started. They started to send... Look, they're destroying our country.' She was crying so much, she could hardly talk. We started to see all those scary images, videos of bombs and rockets falling all across Ukraine during the night. We were both in deep shock.

We didn't really know where we were. It felt like someone close to you had died, but much worse. We were in a daze, disconnected from the world, couldn't process what was happening. I couldn't eat or drink. We spent hours and hours watching TV and checking in with family and friends, wondering what might happen next. My grandfather, we found out, was in a hospital in Kyiv not far from where the bombs had come down on the first day of invasion. Luckily we managed to get someone to pick him up and drive him to Radomyshl, my home town, two hours to the west.

I had terrible dreams. I hardly slept. During the day, we spent hours watching TV, looking at social media and checking on family and friends on the phone. Meanwhile, life carried on as normal outside in Manchester, which made the situation even tougher to deal with. My wife and I didn't speak a lot to each other at that stage. Putting our feelings into words would have made them even more painful. Most of all, I couldn't believe this was actually happening.

It was incredibly hard for me to concentrate on football in those first few days, when it looked as though Kyiv might be surrounded from three sides and they came to kill President Zelensky. Friends told me Russian troops were trying to enter Radomyshl and were hiding in the woods, looking to kill civilians in their cars and take all their belongings. Malyn, a neighbouring town, was attacked with missiles. I would get into the car to drive home from the training ground and forget where I was going. My head wasn't there. And I was crying a lot. The tears just burst out of me, from one minute to the next. I couldn't stop thinking about my home town, where I grew up and knew every stone, every tree, every person living there. I imagined it all being wiped from the earth.

Soon, our worst fears turned into reality. Vlada and I started hearing awful stories. People were getting killed, women were being raped. This happened to friends of friends, normal people with normal lives. Those who escaped unharmed lost everything. Their houses were getting smashed to pieces or looted. TVs, washing machines… The Russians stole everything. They even killed our dogs and ate them. I cannot even begin to describe how I feel about them. 'Hate' is not a strong enough word.

Pep Guardiola left me out of the game against Everton on the 26th. He talked to me and knew that I wasn't quite in the right frame of mind to play. My head simply wasn't there. He understood it. The support from my team-mates and everyone at Everton – where my international team-mate Vitaliy Mykolenko plays – was immensely uplifting. They had Ukrainian flags wrapped around their shirts and we had the flag printed on our pre-match jackets. In the ground, there were 'We stand with Ukraine' banners and messages of solidarity on the screen. I can't thank everyone involved enough for that. To see that people cared made the pain a little easier to bear for me. I didn't feel alone.

Against Peterborough in the FA Cup three days later, it was a great honour to wear the City armband. Fernandinho, who had of course played for Shakhtar Donetsk, like me, approached me in the hotel before the game and told me that he and Pep Guardiola had decided I should skipper the team. It was so kind of them. The whole team showed they were with me in those dark days. I was so lucky to be part of such an amazing club. They all rallied behind me, from Pep down to the kit man. Every day, someone came up to me and asked how I was.

The club were absolutely brilliant. Rodri made a huge donation straight away. Fernandinho later auctioned off the shirt he wore for his final game – the 3-2 win against Aston Villa that clinched the title for us – and City agreed to let Andrei Kravchuk, a refugee from Ukraine, train with the Under-23s for two months. One of the staff invited the entire family of a physio to stay with him. The club doctor told me he would take in any orphans. And then there was Bob, a 71-year-old who has been a City fan since he was six years old. He drove a lorry with medical supplies from Manchester to Ukraine. What a guy. I would like to thank them all from the bottom of my heart.

I also felt the support in the streets of Manchester. I met a kid in a shop; he was maybe ten years old. He said to me, 'We all pray for your country. Hopefully things will work out fine.' I immediately cried when I heard that; I just couldn't help it. Another time I saw this boy, I think he was from the Czech Republic, with a temporary Ukraine tattoo on his shoulder. I often saw cars with Ukraine flags on them, too. These are just little things, but they meant so much to me and everyone back home in Ukraine. They show that the world is standing with us.

Playing football was a distraction, but when you're back home in your house and exposed to all those pictures and the endless stories of suffering, the sadness can be overwhelming. In the end, though, you have two options. You can either continue to walk around as a zombie, zoned out and only half alive, your head filled with dark thoughts about the things that are happening in your country. Or you can do your best to help your country within your means, whether that's by sending money, winter clothes, packing bags or using your connections to help the war effort.

My initial reaction was to go back and fight or volunteer. We all wanted to be there, defending our country. That's our Ukrainian mentality. We are born with it. But then I talked to all the other Ukrainian players who were abroad, and we agreed we could be much more helpful to our people from outside the country. We made a vow that we would carry on playing football, to represent our country as best as possible and use this opportunity to speak out, to make the world aware of what's happening. I'm not a politician. I can't go to the UK parliament and do a speech. Who am I to talk? But in sports and in football, we have the chance to tell our story. And we decided we needed to use it. This is our duty. It's on our shoulders.

It's not just footballers, by the way. I know plenty of Ukrainians who left the country years ago before the war but who have never felt more Ukrainian and are doing anything to help from afar. Our country is sticking together like never before. Friends, family, even people who are much older than me say they cannot remember us being so united. Every Ukrainian is trying to make a positive impact in his or her own way. We are all working together. Not because we want to take over any land that's not ours. We just want to protect ourselves and our home. I'm very proud of how we have responded as a country. We help each other, we support each other, we will not stop. This is our strongest power.

For a while, I used to be in touch with some of the people I know from my time at Ufa. One or two of them texted me when the invasion started. 'I'm so sorry, Alex, but we can't do anything.' Of course you can. But staying silent means you support what's happening. The small circle of friends I had there has dwindled away. That's been very disappointing.

I can think of only a handful of prominent Russians who have spoken out against the war. I'm really frustrated and angry that the vast majority of sportspeople have been utterly quiet. They have massive audiences, a lot of followers, and know exactly what's going on – especially if they live abroad and don't just get their information from Russian state TV. Why won't they speak up and try to stop this?

Don't tell me they are scared. Don't tell me this bullshit that people used to tell me, 'Oh, we are scared because we can go to prison and we will get banned from competing and so on.' I don't believe it. Maybe they are scared, because we see pictures on social media of Russians being taken to prison if they protest. But look at footballers in particular, or anyone with a big platform. Can you believe that, if all of them posted something on Instagram at the same time saying: 'Guys, we are against the war, we need to stop it,' they would all be arrested? Of course they would not. And it's such a shame that they say nothing.

There is an ex-football player, Igor Denisov. He is a Zenit St Petersburg legend. He played for Lokomotiv Moscow, used to be the captain of the Russian national football team. Four months after the war started, he gave an interview on YouTube, calling the invasion 'a complete horror' and 'a catastrophe'. He said, 'What are we doing, fighting our neighbours?' He wrote to Putin three days after it started, begging him to stop. He said he would retire from football immediately if he was still playing, out of protest, because this was not acceptable. In the interview, he said he might be killed or put in jail for his words. But nothing happened to him. Nothing at all. That's why I find it hard not to judge other Russian footballers who could have done the same.

I didn't hear anyone saying, 'It's my dream to play in the Champions League, it's my dream to play in the World Cup for Russia, so let's please stop doing all these bullshit things and let everyone enjoy their lives.' I will never understand it. Footballers have huge audiences and are desperate to play at the highest level in international football. Now they are not allowed to, maybe for a reason? So speak up. Say something.

Maybe they support what's happening or maybe they just don't care. They don't hear the sirens our people can hear every single day, every single night. They don't see bombs falling on their own houses, killing their families. They just carry on living their lives because for them, football aside, very little has changed. They can't fly directly to Europe on holiday any more; they have to go via Istanbul or Dubai. But that's really it. Unfortunately, I have come to realise that waiting for them to take a stand is a waste of time. They haven't done it until now. They won't do it in the future, either.

I had a chat on Instagram about the situation with one of the most famous athletes in Russia. I won't mention his name. I explained to him what was happening in Ukraine. In the end, he stopped replying to me. Perhaps I should have expected that, but it was disappointing to see such indifference from people that used to call us their brothers and sisters not long ago. He didn't personally invade Ukraine, sure. But it was your country, your people. And you keep silent. You are not talking about it at all. Not one post, not one picture that might make people in Russia sit up and wonder what it is they're doing.

We need to live in a peaceful world. But we're not. We're living in a world that's wild. What's the difference between us and animals eating each other in the jungle? What's the point of having nations, borders and passports if from one day to the next someone can decide they no longer believe in that and makes the lives of millions of people a misery? Sometimes I wake up and can't believe that we are in the 2020s. We seem to have learned nothing from history and thousands of years of wars.

We shouldn't lose belief in the Russian population, in the civilians. I hope they will eventually wake up and say 'enough' to all the crimes being perpetrated by their government and soldiers. But two and a half years into this nightmare, we are still waiting. Our so-called brothers haven't come to help us. They have come to destroy us.

This is another harsh lesson for all of us. We need to teach our kids and the next generation who our neighbours really are. They might not all agree with their country waging war on us, they might one day feel ashamed, but for the time being they all seem to be following orders without question. 'Why did you come here, raping and killing people?' 'Oh, sorry, I was just following orders. I don't know why I came here, but they told me to.'

I'm not talking about the people at the top, those who make the decisions. I have nothing but contempt for them. I'm talking about ordinary people. It's obvious to me that they have been turned into zombies, watching one TV channel all their lives and believing it all. A friend of mine told me about this older woman who lived in Kharkiv when the war broke out. She was Russian. When the Russians started bombing the city, her granddaughter travelled from Germany to get her out. She refused to go. She was convinced the Ukrainians were bombing Kharkiv, because that's what Russian media was telling her. I appreciate that people have a hard time understanding reality, having been brainwashed for years, but it's not an excuse for me. We are living in a world where information is freely available. Go listen to a few different perspectives and then make up your mind what's right or wrong. Don't just sit on the sofa and swallow the lies they're feeding you.

I grew up believing those who do bad things have to pay for it, that there's some natural justice. I don't know if I still believe it, even if I want to. It seems to me that the more people you kill, the easier it is to get away with it. Countries are still buying Russian gas and oil, investing in their war and all that violence. But I want to hold on to the idea that there will be a reckoning. One day, those responsible for this hell on earth will be held responsible. They must be held responsible. Until such a time, I would close up that country altogether and not let any of them go abroad. I would keep them separate from the rest of the world, because they are terrorists.

10

North London Calling

In the Champions League, we lost in the semi-final to Real Madrid, despite playing an amazing first leg where we were leading 3-1, then 4-2 before Karim Benzema's penalty to make it 4-3 gave us some work to do, going to the Bernabéu. And there we were, 1-0 up until the 90th minute and pretty much through, when somehow they scored twice in a minute to take it to extra time, and then they won a penalty in the 93rd minute to win the tie 3-1. Somehow, Real Madrid always find a way.

Half the dressing room were in tears after the game. It was just so hard to accept. To be in this position, and then to get knocked out, you might see that once every ten years. Somebody showed me a picture from TV with a graphic that had us going through with a probability of 99 per cent in the 90th minute. And yet Madrid still won. Crazy.

After a game like that, there's no need to say much. Everybody knows that this was a freak event. It's super hard to find any meaningful words. But Pep went over to the players after the final whistle and he said, 'You will be there again. You will be there again. You will be there again.' He kept repeating that same sentence, as much to himself as to the players. But it did have an effect. It got you thinking that this wasn't the end.

For once it was all about the league title for us that year, having been knocked out of the Carabao Cup by West Ham in October and then losing 3-2 against Liverpool in the semi-final of the FA Cup. Again it was a case of Liverpool win, Man City win, week after week in the Premier League. From December on, we lost a game to Tottenham, and drew with Southampton, Crystal Palace and Liverpool, but otherwise won every game until May. Liverpool struggled over Christmas, drawing twice and losing at Leicester, but after that they kept on winning. There was just a point in it until, with three games to go, they drew at home to Spurs and we had a three-point lead. The title was so close for us now. We only had to beat West Ham and Aston Villa to be sure. But it turns out nothing is ever simple.

At West Ham we were 2-0 down at half-time. Our title was slipping away. We knew Liverpool would punish any weakness. But we had never lost the title from a position like this, where it was in our hands. Jack Grealish scored after the break and then Vladimír Coufal deflected in a Riyad Mahrez free kick. In the end, we should have won the game, but the draw meant that going into the last day of the season, we were a point ahead and knew that if we beat Aston Villa, the title was ours.

And that last game would become the perfect finale to my City career. I think the best emotions I ever experienced in football were that day against Aston Villa. Crazy emotions. Maybe if we had won the game 4-0, it wouldn't have felt like that. But the way we won! I can't imagine how it felt being a fan watching that game and the Liverpool game.

I started on the bench and Liverpool were 1-0 down after three minutes. Someone from the staff behind said, 'Oh, Liverpool are 1-0 down.' So for us, that meant even a draw was fine. But soon it was 1-1 at Anfield and then we conceded to Villa, a Matty Cash goal, and it was like 2019 at Brighton all over again. 'Oh, oh, we need to score.' In theory, even if Liverpool drew and we lost, we were still okay because of the goal difference. But you knew you couldn't rely on that. And that first half was painful. We tried so many things, but we couldn't even get close to the goal. I remember we didn't have a proper chance.

I came on for the second half but although things were better, we couldn't score. And when Philippe Coutinho scored for Villa on 67 minutes for 2-0, you feared the worst, that we would hand the title to Liverpool on the last day. It seemed unthinkable, but now we had so much to do. At least we were creating chances, and there is always a way with Pep's teams.

İlkay came on as a sub on 68 minutes and, finally, on 76 minutes, we had the breakthrough when he scored with a header. Two minutes later, I made maybe my most decisive impact for City. I received the ball on the left, cut inside the defender, drove into the penalty area and laid it back for Rodri. Those shots from the edge of the box, low and accurate, they're his trademark. Like in the Champions League final in 2023, he hit this one sweetly, directly into the bottom corner just beyond the hand of Villa keeper Robin Olsen. The relief was huge and the noise unbelievable. We were top! But if Liverpool won, they would overtake us. And though it was still 1-1 at Anfield, we knew they would win (they did, 3-1). So we couldn't stop. It was a couple of minutes later, on 81 minutes, that İlkay's winner went in. Only then could you begin to feel secure, and the euphoria and relief all around the Etihad was off the scale.

When the final whistle went, I was on the far side of the pitch, furthest away from the tunnel, so I had no chance of avoiding the crowd invasion. The pitch was so full, you couldn't even see a patch of green on the TV shots. Imagine what it was like for me, fighting my way from the far side to the dressing room! It took around 15 minutes. People are all over you, jumping on you, hugging you. You just have to battle your way through. Once in the dressing room, there were crazy emotions everywhere, the best ever. When you are more involved and have played the key games, you feel a bit differently. I can only compare it with the first Premier League title, where I didn't play much, just eight Premier League games. Of course I was overwhelmed then to win my first Premier League title. But as the years went by, the wins felt different, more important. And that last year was the best feeling of all. Now I had truly earned my medal.

The celebrations were pretty raucous that night, or so I was told. Three months after the start of the war, I wasn't in the mood for wild festivities, and we had the key World Cup qualification games coming up a few days later. I left the party quite early. But on my way home I did stop for a very special treat, the kind of indulgence I've only allowed myself a handful of times since becoming a footballer: a takeaway from McDonald's.

***

We were supposed to play our World Cup qualification play-offs in March, but the games were postponed to June, due to the war. For the players based in Ukraine, that was difficult – they had no competitive matches for more than three months, just one very long training camp with a few friendlies. Borussia Mönchengladbach (Germany), Empoli (Italy) and Rijeka (Croatia) invited the team to play charity games, with the proceeds going to Ukraine, but those weren't games against international teams and you can't really gain match sharpness that way in any case. But what the team might have lacked in sharpness, we made up for with motivation. You could feel the determination in the group, and also a strong patriotic spirit. Whereas in the past some would have listened to Russian pop or spoken Russian – the first language of those who grew up in the east and south of the country – we listened only to Ukrainian music in the dressing room and spoke only Ukrainian to each other.

Everyone dreams of playing in the World Cup when they grow up, but we didn't play for that. All we thought about was making our people happy, and to remind the whole world again about Ukraine and what was happening to us. Four months into the conflict, you could sense that some were starting to forget about it. We didn't go to Scotland to play a game. We went on a mission, to give our people a bit of respite from war, to bring some good emotions to those living under bombs and all those rockets in the air, and to show that, as a country, we would not be cowed.

A lot of us had tears in our eyes during the national anthem at Hampden Park, especially when the crowd cheered us. Kieran Tierney, my Arsenal team-mate, later told me, 'Fucking hell, I felt like we were playing away,' because the stadium was almost yellow. We put our heart and soul into the game, but the key was keeping a cool head and not getting overwhelmed by our emotions. You can't just rely on effort at this level, you need to prepare. In the run-up to the match, we practised defending against 'second balls', knockdowns from long balls to the strikers. After a wild opening spell with lots of tackles flying in, we were in control. We showed our class and won 3-1.

'They went out. They fought. They persevered. They won. Because they are Ukrainians!' President Zelensky wrote, thanking us for 'two hours of happiness' that the country was no longer used to. Every player also received hundreds of personal messages after the final whistle. A lot of them came from soldiers who had somehow managed to see the game between bouts of fighting at the front. 'We played for those who fight in the trenches, who fight with their last drop of blood,' our manager, Oleksandr Petrakov, told the press. 'We also play for people at home who are suffering every day.'

Next, we travelled to Wales for a game four days later. One more win, and we'd be at the World Cup! We put up a big flag with handwritten messages from soldiers in our dressing room at the Millennium Stadium. The Welsh Football Association kindly donated 100 tickets to Ukrainian refugees. There were about 1,800 of our supporters in the ground, but we played like the home team. We had 26 shots at goal, but we simply couldn't score. Their goalkeeper, Wayne Hennessey, said afterwards that he had played the game of his life. He was 35 at the time, so that tells the story. We dominated, but conceded a deflected goal and lost 1-0. It's football, these things can happen, but it was very painful. I felt we deserved to be in Qatar in a sporting sense, that we had done enough to get there. Everyone was very down.

This was the second World Cup we had missed out on, after failing to qualify for Russia in 2018. In a tough group with Finland, Turkey, Iceland and Croatia, we were in the running until the last game of the qualifiers, at home to Luka Modrić's side – the team that would finish runners-up in Moscow a few months later. We lost 2-0 in Kyiv. Andrej Kramarić scored two identical goals, two headers. I was still young, though, and didn't feel that disappointment too strongly. Besides that, relations with Russia had deteriorated a lot at that stage. There were rumours we might boycott the tournament in case of qualification, and there were also concerns about the safety of our supporters in Russia. The team definitely played to qualify and tried, but we will never know what would have happened. The bottom line is that not going to Russia didn't feel nearly as bad as not making it to Qatar four years later, because this had become much bigger than football for us. Failure to qualify hurt because we felt we had let the nation down. We were hugely frustrated and sad that we weren't able to bring a bit of happiness to our country to relieve the pain, even if for a few days.

Playing at the biggest competition in football, with millions of people watching, and visitors from all corners of the world in the stadiums, would have been a great chance to remind everyone not to forget about us. But we had to carry on spreading the message regardless. The moment we lost, we made the point that the much more important part of our story must continue to be at the forefront of people's minds, especially in Europe. 'We just want you to understand what is happening back home,' our manager pleaded with reporters in Cardiff. 'We have war raging all over the country. We have children and women dying on a daily basis. Our infrastructure is being ruined by Russian barbarians. The Russians want to hurt us, but the Ukrainians are resisting and defending their land. We just want your support.' It's not enough for us to speak about what is happening to Ukraine. You have to scream about it.

***

I had a contract with City until 2024, but I wasn't sure what the future held, because two years out is about the time when you start to renegotiate. During my holidays, Txiki Begiristain called me into his office and said there were a few clubs calling and asking about me, but he didn't know what to tell them, what I wanted. I said, 'Listen, I'll be honest with you, my target was always to stay with City. If you want me, I'm more than happy to stay and fight for my place and help the team as much as I can. I'm so happy in this place.' The conversation was five minutes, no more than that. Then a few days later, I got a couple of calls from different Premier League managers asking me about the situation, how it was. And to all of them, I just said my priority was to stay at City. But, of course, you never know what's going to happen. Maybe Pep is going to say, 'Well, Alex, I don't need you any more.'

And that's when Mikel Arteta called me. I had always said, 'Guys, if one day I leave City and I stay in the Premier League, I will only go to one manager: Mikel.' I used to say this whenever there were rumours. And then he called me, asked me the situation, what I was feeling. My response was exactly the same as to the rest, that my priority was to stay at City, but you never know. And then I told him what I had always said to my friends: 'Mikel, if I ever leave City, there is only one other manager in this league I will play for. You know which manager this is! You know!' And so we were laughing, because he knew, as City assistant manager, it had been a bit emotional for me when he left; he had been so close to me. At the end of our chat, he said: 'Okay, let's see what's going to happen.'

I came back for pre-season with City, was training for a week in Manchester, and that was when the guys upstairs at City called my agent and said, 'Look, the situation is that we've reached an agreement with Arsenal. And we're letting you know that we're not going to extend Alex's contract after 2024. Our priority is to re-sign a new contract with Rodri and Foden, but not Alex. So, now it's down to you, guys. You're free to negotiate a deal with Arsenal.'

I was very surprised to hear that. It was quite an unusual turn of events. Normally, when someone wants to sign you, they call you. They're asking if you're happy to join. You speak about contracts. And then, while you fix those details, they will go to the club. It might not be strictly by the book, because you're not supposed to contact players under contract with another club, but that's how it's usually done.

I talked to another City player about my situation at the time. His was a classic case: he had already reached an agreement with the new club, but they couldn't find an agreement between the clubs. And the player wanted to leave. His desire to leave was not crazy, but he was quite okay to move on. But in the end, they couldn't find the agreement between the clubs and he stayed at City. So knowing all this, knowing how it works normally, I got a feeling they didn't really want to keep me. I hadn't expected the Villa game to have been my last one for City. But that's life. I had to move forward.

While all this was happening, Mikel and Edu came to my house in Manchester. Gabi Jesus joined us as well, as a surprise guest. He had already signed for Arsenal a few days earlier. Him being there was a smart touch from the Mister. He knew how close we were. It was a tight-knit group at City, but my relationship with Gabi was particularly strong. I've known him longer than my wife! I love this guy so much; he's such a good friend.

We had a really good chat between the four of us. I remember we sat outside in the garden. It was a beautiful day. We talked about the role they envisaged for me, playing on the left of defence, but moving inside as an extra midfielder quite often. Mikel mentioned that he liked my versatility and that I could also start as a midfielder. To be honest, I would have played in goal too, if he wanted me to. We also talked about my role off the pitch. Mikel wanted experienced players who had won big trophies to help his side take the next step. The three of them also told me about their commitment to the project, the way they were pushing each other inside the camp. I knew it wasn't just talk. I had already spoken to Gabi about Arsenal in the past and he had said the same: 'Everyone is really nice, an amazing group of people. We can do big things as a club.'

I believed them, because I had felt it too. Even from a distance, 200 miles away in Manchester, I could see that

Arsenal's time was coming. Or maybe I should say: I could smell it. They had a young team, full of hungry and talented players doing amazing things – and Mikel. He played the most important role in my decision. I had known him for a while, had worked with him at Manchester City. From the very first day, I knew he would be a very good head coach in the future. He sees football in a very specific way, and you could see it in his Arsenal side. They had an identity, a style. His style. I wanted to be a part of it, desperately.

You could immediately see the discipline and structure he brought to the club. A lot of things he was doing there were similar to those I had encountered at Man City. His vision wasn't something I had to buy into with blind faith; I knew exactly what it looked like. And I also knew already how good he was as a manager and person, a really hard worker who pushed players individually to get better and more consistent all the time. I had learned so much from him.

Basically, my mind was made up there and then that I would join. I didn't need a lot of convincing. When the manager comes to see you and asks you to help him put his footballing ideas into practice, when he knows exactly what you can bring to the team and tells you, 'You are the one I need,' you say to yourself, 'Why wouldn't I go?' Gabi was also pushing me, gently. He said, 'Zinna, you have to make a decision, like I did. I can tell you, I couldn't be happier with it.' I saw he really meant it. But I told them I had to talk it over with my wife first.

Then they went back to London. I felt like going with them but couldn't just go with my emotions. Vlada and I were up all night talking through all the pros and cons, what we had to do if we wanted to leave or if we wanted to stay. What were we going to do? But I was still with City. I had to do my job, I had to respect my contract. I went to training the next day and tried to put my thoughts to one side as best I could. When I came back that afternoon, I opened the door and saw the whole corridor was full of red things. Mikel had sent a mountain of stuff from the fan shop: Arsenal baby bottles, Arsenal baby dresses, hats, scarves, shirts.

And there was a letter from Mikel. 'Welcome to the Arsenal family,' it read. This was the first time a manager and a club had really taken this much time and care to impress on me how much they wanted me to play for them and paid so much attention to me, down to the details and that nice idea of sending stuff from the fan shop. I never felt appreciated like that before in my career. I wouldn't say it was an easy decision, but it was a quick and obvious one in the end. On the one hand, there was a club who told me they wouldn't extend my contract, and on the other a manager, sporting director and player travelling to meet me, and showing a strong desire to get me in. You don't say no to that kind of approach.

As a player, having the trust and confidence of your manager is absolutely key. It's a huge source of power and confidence to know you are important to the manager and for the team. You draw huge motivation from that.

And it was Arsenal! The team I had always watched as a kid, the team I supported. I loved watching Dennis Bergkamp, Thierry Henry, Cesc Fàbregas, Robin van Persie … what a fantastic side. There was no other option I considered that summer. In the Premier League, I wasn't prepared to look at any other club after playing for the best team of the decade. The experience of going on loan at PSV had also taught me a valuable lesson. I vowed to myself that I would never again join a club where the manager didn't really want me. It's not enough that you speak to the sporting director or the CEO. Their opinion ultimately doesn't matter if the manager doesn't like you. To be clear: I'm only blaming myself for things not working out at Eindhoven, no one else. But you have to give yourself the best possible chance to succeed. Once I had spoken to Mikel, I knew it was the right call, and I was certain I would have no regrets whatsoever.

As the deal between the clubs was only 95 per cent done, I flew out with City to Houston for their pre-season in the US. Everyone knew I was going to join Arsenal and all the players were having a laugh. 'Oh, so nice of you to still be with us!' 'Please, please don't leave me, Zinny!' 'Come on man, what are you doing here? You're asking them for more money, is that it?' 'You fight for every penny, don't you? Good for you, take all their money!' Those kind of jokes. I had an amazing relationship with these guys and still have it now.

And while we were on tour in the USA, the news came from my agent that we had agreed the money and I had to meet up with Arsenal, who were also in the USA. The contracts were all signed but, before I went, there was a team dinner with all the players and staff. And when I came in, Pep asked for silence, then he started to talk. To be honest, I couldn't believe what he said. I'm an emotional person. If I watch *Titanic*, I'll be crying every time, I swear. So I couldn't hold back the tears that day.

'Alex,' Pep said, 'before you even arrived, a guy called me and said, "There is this blond guy, good player, decent qualities. He might be useful for the development squad." And when this blond guy joined us, we were trying to send him out on loan. Every transfer window we were saying, "Go on loan, it would be good for you." But this blond guy always used to say, "I'm going to stay, I'm going to fight for my place, I'm happy to stay." And this guy, because of this attitude, he convinced me that he's ready to play for this team. And his behaviour every single day convinced me even more. He never had a sad face during this period. Even when he deserved to play but he didn't play, he still was working so hard. Alex, that guy was you. And that's why you're an example to everyone here.' It was so emotional. I could never have expected it. He made me feel like a member of the family. Then I shook everyone's hands, hugged everyone. I didn't even have time to have a proper dinner. So I said goodbye to everyone like this, then went to my room.

In the morning, I had my flight and felt like I had already said my goodbyes, so I was just going to leave.

I was in the lobby, checking out at reception, when suddenly Pep was calling. 'Alex,' he said. 'Wait! You were going to leave without saying goodbye to me?!' So he sat me down again, we chatted, and again he was saying it was a pleasure to work with me. And again it was emotional for me. I couldn't hold my emotions in. I didn't cry, but I guess he saw there were some tears in my eyes.

I knew I had been so lucky to have these five seasons. When they brought me there from FC Ufa, my plan was that I would play for Manchester City. Their plan was just to send me out on loans and maybe if I did something incredible, maybe I would have a chance. But that was the least likely option. The most likely was that they would sell me to someone else without having played for City. But in the end, I had five amazing seasons, four Premier League medals, four Carabao Cup medals, an FA Cup medal and a Champions League final. Maybe I would have played more games at another club, but how can I regret this? To be part of perhaps the best team in the world in that period. I didn't get a present when I left, but that wasn't necessary. The experience and all those happy moments at City were the best gift any footballer could ever hope for.

Being at City was an extraordinary education and a privilege. I was aware of that every single day. But after I left, with perspective, it became even clearer to me how incredible it had been. And the moment I truly knew it? It was when Manchester City won the treble, in June 2023, beating Inter in the Champions League final. A few days later, in the middle of those celebrations, I got a call from

Pep. 'Alex,' he said. 'You are a big part of this. You may not be here. But you helped to make this happen.' I just told him, 'Listen, I truly realise now how special it was.' It was a very moving moment. But by then there was a new coach and a new club in my life.

11

Gold

Three years earlier, Aleksandar Kolarov left us on the US tour to go to Roma. Now it was my turn to finally part ways. I boarded a plane to Florida, where Arsenal were staying ahead of their match against Orlando City. I was so happy to see everyone and shake everyone's hands. 'Finally you're here,' Mikel said to me. 'Come.'

But before I could sign, I had to undergo medical tests. I must have spent about four hours lying still in the MRI scanner. Not a pleasant experience. Then I could finally put pen to paper and slip on the Arsenal shirt for the first time. Well, not quite for the first time. The club's media department found an old photo of me wearing a Gunners top as a skinny kid at the Shakhtar academy and posted it online. I remember how good I had felt that day. It really suited me, I thought.

I guess I wasn't the only one. Somebody else had liked the look of me in that shirt, too. Remember that Youth

Champions League game against Arsenal in 2014? We lost 3-1. Two months after the game, I got a call from an agent called Sandor Varga. He said, 'Alex, I have a very good connection with Arsène Wenger. He called me after your game against Arsenal. He really wants to see you in the club – in the first team.' I was speechless; my jaw was on the floor. When I gathered my thoughts after a few seconds, I said: 'This is probably a joke. Someone is having a laugh here.' Varga insisted it was true, though. 'Of course I'll go,' I told him at the end of the conversation. For one reason or another, it never happened.

I had sort of forgotten about this whole thing until Wenger came to the Emirates in December 2022 to watch us beat West Ham 3-1. He hadn't been to the ground in over four years. He walked up to me in the dressing room after the final whistle and I shook his hand. I had never met him in person before. I wanted to find out if there was anything to that story. 'Mister, eight years ago I played for Shakhtar Donetsk in a Youth League game against Arsenal…' I said, cautiously. He interrupted me. 'Yes, it was at Boreham Wood. Arsenal won 3-1. And after 20 minutes, I pointed at you and said to Sandor: "I need this guy."' It was all true. Incredible. I sometimes imagine what would have happened if I had joined the first team as a 17-year-old.

Would it have worked out? Serge Gnabry, who scored us against us that day, broke into the first team at that age but was then sent out on loan to West Bromwich Albion. Their manager said, 'Serge has come here to play games but he just hasn't been for me, at the moment, at that level to play the games.' He had to return to Germany to make it as a pro. God's plan. There's a plan for all of us, our destiny. What happened in 2014, happened for a reason. Or perhaps I should say: it didn't happen for a reason.

Signing for Arsenal was a dream. I know it's a cliché; every new player says it. But in my case, it's really true. They were my team as a kid. We didn't have too many television channels at home but I always found a way to see their games, as well as Barcelona with Messi, and, if I was allowed to stay up late, the Champions League. Watching these amazing players was an inspiration, but I only realised that years later. Growing up in Ukraine, I hadn't even dared to dream about playing for Arsenal one day. The mere idea of it felt preposterous. Now I was there, holding up a shirt with my name on it. I just couldn't stop smiling.

I celebrated signing my contract by getting on stage in the team hotel and singing a song in front of all the players and staff for my initiation later that evening. 'Friday', by Riton x Nightcrawlers, was the tune of my choice. But perhaps 'tune' isn't quite the right word in this context. Judge for yourself. You can see the clip on social media, as well as, shall we say, the less than enthusiastic reaction of my new team-mates. I was quite relieved they didn't send me straight back to City after that.

From my time in Manchester, I knew the Mister would be able to help me learn as a footballer. I had to take this opportunity. He's also just a really great guy, one of those you can be really open with. Players often have a closer relationship to the assistant coach than the manager, who keeps more of a distance, but we still had that connection. Everyone is different, but I like to talk to people I have many things in common with, and I could talk to Mikel about football for hours.

The Mister wanted me to inject a winning mentality into the dressing room, and I tried to do that straight away. I told the players on my first day, 'We can win the Premier League.' I saw in some of the faces they didn't quite believe me. They didn't believe it yet, in any case. Maybe because they were still so young and hadn't figured out how good they were. They also hadn't won anything at Arsenal, apart from the players who had lifted the FA Cup in 2020. When you haven't done something before, it can be hard to envision yourself doing something, whereas winning has a self-perpetuating effect. That's why experience is very important in football. Having lived through the highs and lows prepares you for those situations. You gain confidence from knowing you can deal with those moments.

I didn't tell them we could be champions because I was looking for a reaction. I was truly convinced this group were good enough. After my first training session with the team, I remember talking to one of the assistants and saying, 'I swear to you, the quality we have is incredible.' I said the same to Gabi. 'This team – wow! We can achieve something big if we're going to believe in ourselves, you know?'

Gabi helped me a lot in those first days because he had been with the club for a little while already. We get on really well, even though we make for an odd couple in terms of looks and background. It had been like that at City. We're almost the same age, and he's such a lovely guy. You spend more time with your team-mates than your family during the season, travelling, playing cards, on the pitch… It's so important that you have someone that you enjoy talking to, somebody who listens. When I arrived in Manchester, Fernandinho was my guide, he took great care of me. He spoke my language from his time at Shakhtar. I became good friends with him and Gabi.

There's something about the Brazilians in general that I admire. Their mentality is so different. They just love football and enjoy every minute. I love that. They sort of adopted me, and I was made an honorary member of the Brazilian and Portuguese group. When the team was split up for exercises along nationalities, there was an English group, a 'rest of the world' and the Portuguese speakers. I was always with them. 'Half Ukrainian, half Brazilian,' they called me. It's still like that at Arsenal.

I had played against most of these boys already many times in the league and felt we sort of knew each other. They were all quite young and easy-going. It was easy to find common ground. They made me feel like family right away. The atmosphere in the camp was amazing, very buzzy and happy but also very driven and motivated. Football-wise, they were even better than I thought they would be.

I was surprised a lot by Gabriel Martinelli; I didn't realise how quick and relentless he was. Bukayo Saka,

I knew him well already, of course, but still: the potential of that guy? Ridiculous. An absolute joke. William Saliba? I honestly didn't know who he was but I was in total shock after just one session with him. I don't think I've ever seen a defender like him before, the confidence he has on the ball, the calmness without it. He's always in the right spaces, which isn't normal for a player of such a young age. He looks like he was born to defend. Even the best strikers in the world did not faze him at all. And Martin Ødegaard? I knew he was already a mega talent at 15, when he moved to Real Madrid, but he had gone to a completely different level since coming to the Emirates. He's the perfect blend of technique and determination. The way he runs at people with the ball is frightening for opponents. Thomas Partey as well. What a player. I never realised how amazing he was and the qualities he has. He's been unlucky with injuries, but I was so impressed with him.

Just 24 hours after joining up with the group, Mikel put me in the starting XI for the friendly against Chelsea. It was a really memorable night for me, especially in light of the emphatic scoreline. We beat them 4-0; it was great. The ground in Orlando was full of Arsenal supporters. I wish I had the words to explain how I felt, actually playing for the team I had followed for years as a kid. But really, it was indescribable.

And it got better. A few minutes into my competitive debut, away to Crystal Palace, Arsenal supporters were singing 'Zinchenko – always believe in your soul!' to the tune of Spandau Ballet's 'Gold'. Vlada sat in the Selhurst Park stand and couldn't believe the fans were chanting my name. Some players turn out for clubs for years before anyone comes up with a song for them, but I had played for Arsenal for only a few minutes! I felt so honoured. We couldn't have hoped for a more beautiful welcome. I will forever be grateful for that.

London is a big draw for many professional players. They want the shops, the clubs, the restaurants. But I don't care about all that. My routine doesn't look much different to the one I had in Manchester: training ground, hotel, Emirates or away ground, back home to relax and start again. I will go out to dinner once every two weeks to a restaurant, but Manchester had nice places too. Moving to London was perhaps more of a change for my family. They had to get used to new nurseries and so on. But things didn't really change for me. I'm here to play football, and enjoy the game, not to enjoy the lifestyle.

There's a strong family vibe at Arsenal and Manchester City; that's a big part of being a successful club. Arsenal have a bigger worldwide audience, whereas City have probably the best facilities in the league. Everything is compact, the training ground is next to the stadium. But they're both huge clubs that are brilliantly run. Perhaps the biggest difference I noticed is that at Arsenal, you are part of the fabric of the club's history, while at City, the most successful time of the club is obviously right now, in the new Pep era.

You are constantly being reminded of past achievements at Arsenal. You see all the trophies that have been won before your time here and you often bump into these amazing players. Some players might feel intimidated by that; I take it as an inspiration. It's always good to meet people who have been in the position to win silverware and done so; you can seek out their advice on anything. Besides that, I'm an unashamed fan boy when it comes to former Gunners greats.

I was lucky to play with ex-Arsenal midfielder Emmanuel Frimpong at Ufa. He was surprised when I walked up to him for the phone numbers of Cesc Fàbregas, Robin van Persie and all the other wonderful players he played with. I peppered him with questions about Arsenal every minute. 'Are you a supporter or a professional football player?' he laughed. Well, I'm both. I'm lucky to play for the club I loved well before I could ever imagine kicking a ball for money.

I've been in touch with Gaël Clichy since meeting him at Arsenal in pre-season. Robert Pires is often around. When Tony Adams came to one of the games, I asked club photographer Stuart MacFarlane to introduce us and take a photo as well. The word 'legend' is used too often in football, but he certainly is one. I was aware of his standing before I moved here, having watched plenty of clips of him online. I told Tony that Andriy Shevchenko always said to me he was the toughest opponent he ever played against. Tony just laughed. He's such a good guy. Always ready to make a joke.

Things clicked from the very first moment. We won the two opening games, against Palace (2-0) and Leicester (4-2), and then we travelled to Bournemouth. The Vitality Stadium can be a tricky place to go, but we were out of sight after just 11 minutes. Martin's first goal was all about magic from Gabi. He plucked a really high ball out of the air with the ease of someone picking up an apple in the supermarket, swerved around four players and then played the perfect disguised ball to Martinelli. Martin scored a tap-in on the rebound, then scored again soon after from a cutback from Ben White. Game over.

The moment of the match came in the second half, however. In the aftermath of a free kick, Granit Xhaka passed the ball to William Saliba at the edge of the box. He smashed it first time under the crossbar. My reaction said it all: I went down on my knees, holding my head in disbelief. Is there something this guy can't do?

I've been lucky to play with so many fantastic centre-backs before, but I don't think I've ever seen someone who doesn't just win every tackle but controls the ball in a way that you can immediately recycle it as a team. Most defenders are happy to boot it, but he's like a Rolls-Royce, smooth as butter. The whole friendly against Chelsea: zero mistakes. He never makes any mistakes. He's different class. And then he goes and nonchalantly whacks it into the top corner. I had played 100 Premier League games without a goal, but this guy turns up and scores a screamer with his weaker foot in his third game. I love him so much.

Granit, Gabi Martinelli and I struck up an instant connection as a trio on the left. These sub-teams are very important in Arteta's game. We often move up and down the pitch together and then rotate in the final third to create openings. Mikel showed us a few basketball videos to explain how simple positional changes can disrupt defences, especially if they press the man, not the ball. To play like that needs a lot of detailed training groundwork and video analysis, but most importantly it needs good communication. We've had tactical sessions where the coaching staff didn't give us any input at all, on purpose. They wanted to hear us talking to each other, making sure that all the positions were correctly occupied.

At City, we had plenty of players who could break defensive lines with passes. Pep didn't really demand it of me that much. It was more important that I took up the right spaces on and off the ball, that I marked my man and moved inside to create overloads in the centre. But I wasn't the engine of the team, more like a little part that many didn't really notice.

It's different at Arsenal. That's what I'm demanding of myself in any case. If you look at the team, I'm the fourth oldest, so I can't just be coasting along. I need to drive this team. I need to make a difference. That's why, in games, I'm looking for passes that open up the opposition. But you can't do it by yourself. Passing is a collective skill. The greatest passer in the world can't do anything if he has no options. During training, warm-up and the game itself, you always need to be in touch with your team-mates to make sure you're on the same wavelength. They need to know what they need to do when you have the ball, and you need to know they will do it.

Take Gabi Jesus as an example. An unbelievable player. The quality he has is phenomenal. Maybe he's not scoring as many goals as people are demanding from him. He's not an old-school No. 9 who touches the ball twice to score two goals. He could probably do that, too, but he's too good on the ball for that. It suits him to drop a bit, get more involved. I'm always in touch with him when we play together. I've said to him, 'Gabi, when I'm on the ball, especially without pressure, you're the first player I look for.' Maybe he'll come towards me. Maybe he'll make a run. It doesn't matter, I will try to find him. We have this understanding. He will make the move the second I'm on the ball. It looks like telepathy, but it's really another form of communication. You need that level of understanding in a team.

Routine teaches you to adapt to different situations in a game. It comes automatically; it's muscle memory. If you have enjoyed the right education as a footballer, if you have quality, you can always get on top of any situation. But the form that reaction takes depends on your role.

In my view, holding midfielder is the toughest position on the pitch. Why? Because you have to be in the game every single second. When I'm on the left and the ball is on the other side, far away from me, I need to worry about being in the right position but I know that, most of the time, I'll get a second or two of rest. For a holding midfielder, that's impossible. You are constantly moving. You always have to be somewhere close to the ball, at the right angle to help your team-mate, to give him a solution, close to an opponent as well, ready to engage if you've lost the ball. You need to understand where you need to be at any moment of the game because your position affects everyone else. If you push, everyone needs to push. If you drop, say, between two defenders, to lure out their attackers, the players in front of you need to be ready for the pass.

At City, and now even more so at Arsenal, I often start on the left side of defence but move inside in possession. Pep came up with this hybrid role at Bayern Munich. Philipp Lahm and David Alaba played liked that. Opponents couldn't cope. A player playing two positions at the same time creates big problems for the other side. If I go into the centre to make it a three in midfield, we have the numbers. Their right winger needs to come in to track me. But if he does that, our winger is clear to go up one vs one against their full-back. And our winger will beat their full-back. Job done for me, just by stepping inside. If their winger stays out wide and leaves me to run in midfield, I can draw out opponents and play through them. If I was the opposition manager, I'd struggle to come up with a good solution against that.

So why isn't everyone playing like that, you might ask? Because it's a very difficult idea to make work when you lose the ball. Imagine our move breaks down and the opponent attacks our left side. There might be a lot of space there, as I'm still in the middle trying to get across. You need to reorganise very quickly, because one spot on the pitch is not filled at that moment. We worked very hard in training on that. Either the left-sided central midfielder or the left-sided centre-back need to adapt. They need to be ready for the defensive transition and already think about recovering the ball before we lose it. You need to have very intelligent players to understand that. I was used to it from City, but at Arsenal it was a relatively new concept. It's a hard job and hard work to pull that off. But we got it right more quickly than I anticipated. That proved to me, once more, what an incredibly high calibre of players we have here.

Once the game kicks off, you can hardly hear the manager, if at all. Every game in the Premier League is so fast and fluid that he cannot micromanage every move from the sideline. You need players to coach each other. And that's why playing next to Granit was such a privilege. We used to speak a lot to each other, before the game, during the game and after the game. I think he once said in an interview that he thought, 'Is this guy ever going to shut up?' But I know he appreciated me being so vocal. We were constantly coaching and correcting each other. I told him where I wanted to see him, he told me where he wanted to receive the ball, he told me where we needed to be positioned as a unit and the other way around. We rotated positions a lot, too. Right at the beginning, I told him, 'I will adapt to you. It's easier for me because I can see you ahead of me. You won't see me because I'm too far behind you and you need to turn your head 10,000 times. I will take my cue from you, I will follow you.'

It's like putting a complex puzzle together with a mate while you're both running full tilt. You can't do it in silence. You must hear your team-mate and your team-mate must hear you. We were both very vocal, which is why our build-up process was so successful. He was always receiving the ball in good areas, ready to go forward. That's one of the reasons he played one of the best seasons of his career at Arsenal that year.

I saw a lot of similarities between me and him. Not so much as players – I wish I had his qualities. But he's such an amazing guy off the pitch, too. The way he thinks, the way he does things… He's a role model for me. And the job he was doing was phenomenal. A lot of it is the dirty stuff, the stuff that not many see or notice because it happens off the ball. Off-camera, if you will. The way he protected my side, the left flank, when we lost the ball – he ran like an animal. That's why we didn't have many problems defensively. Granit was like a very important piece inside a Rolex watch. He made it all work and gave others a chance to sparkle. Without him, Arsenal would have never gone to a different level that season.

We were top of the table from August, bar a couple of weeks in October. Until the end of January, we only lost one game, 3-1 at Manchester United. But the way we lost it said a lot about our progress. Gabi Martinelli scored a superb goal, only for it to be ruled out for the softest of touches by Martin on Christian Eriksen in the build-up.

Why VAR got involved there, I'll never know. We dominated the game despite going 1-0 down, scored an equaliser (Bukayo Saka) and then were hit by two Marcus Rashford counter-attacks. It hurt to lose after five wins in a row at the start of the season, but we left Old Trafford convinced we could beat any side, home or away, if we cut out those mistakes. We were genuine title contenders. After so many years in the wilderness, our supporters were buzzing.

In football, good things usually take a bit of time to take shape but with Arsenal, everything seemed to happen at light speed. The quality I saw on my very first day made me hugely optimistic and there was another one of those moments when we beat Tottenham 2-0 away in January. To go to Spurs and win is one thing, but to do it the way we did was quite another. I remember we destroyed them in the first half. Bukayo scored the opener – with a bit of help from their keeper, Hugo Lloris – and he and Martin celebrated by shooting imaginary hoops, in reference to the rotation principles inspired by the NBA. Martin got a second from distance, but it could have been three or four easily. We came into the dressing room and one of the players went up to me and said, 'Bro, we are so fucking good. We dominate the game for fun.' Someone else asked me, 'This is how City play every game, right?' I said, 'Yes, this is how they play every single game. They dominate the opponent no matter what.' That game, every player respected the position, no one lost any silly balls. It was simply an incredible performance against a proper rival.

The only sour note was crashing out of the FA Cup – at the Etihad, of all places. We pushed them hard but couldn't take our chances. The tie was settled by a Nathan Aké goal. I was very down afterwards. Kyle Walker and İlkay Gündoğan making some jokes at my expense after the game didn't help improve my mood, but I forgave them quickly. It's all love between us, due to the many good moments we have shared.

A wise guy once said to me, 'In football, start your game with the right pass, because your first action will always give you a boost and raise your confidence.' That's why I'm always trying to be fully focused on my first action on the pitch. It could be a duel, it could be a pass. It's vital to get that right, especially when you play away at a place where the crowd is loud and they try to unsettle you. Just stay calm and play your game. When you're playing, they will sit down, they won't be loud any more. That's exactly what we did against Tottenham that day. We were on top of them from kick-off, and all you could hear was our own supporters. We shut down their stadium. It was some performance, and we got a sense of how big that win was for our fans. After that game, I was certain we would challenge for the league title.

The next match, 3-2 vs Manchester United, was probably my best one in an Arsenal shirt, and it was a real five goal-thriller on top of that, a very tough game. We scored a wonderfully worked goal that came from the left side – cross from Granit, header from Eddie Nketiah – to equalise after Rashford's opener. Bukayo's shot from distance was unstoppable, but it looked as if we might drop two points when Lisandro Martinez scored with a looping header. Arsenal would not be denied, however. We created tons of chances in the last few minutes and found a breakthrough in stoppage time in a classic move. The ball went from right to left to shift United's defence. Martin deflected my low cross into the path of Eddie, who improvised with a volleyed heel finish.

The stadium exploded. I ran over to the fans to celebrate but almost regretted it. It was so loud, I was afraid my ears might fall off. Seriously: I had never experienced the Emirates like that and I don't think many Arsenal players had either. Later, supporters told me it was the best atmosphere they had witnessed since the club moved there from Highbury in 2006. I guess scoring so late had something to do with it. Nothing is sweeter. Nothing hurts more when you're on the other side.

When we used to play at Arsenal with City, we were aware of the threat they posed as a team. But the crowd were never really much of a factor there, unlike at other places. That's completely changed now. The energy and noise from supporters has become incredible. Honestly, it makes a huge difference to us as players. When you step onto the pitch and feel that electricity, it hits you deep inside and makes you grow in confidence immediately. The opponents also feel it. It's no longer 11 vs 11 out there but 11 vs 60,000. You might think professional players have seen it all before and don't get affected by it, but I promise you: it's important.

That Manchester United match also stuck in my mind for another reason. The build-up had been very special. For Mikel, the game doesn't start in the dressing room – it starts in the team meeting a few hours before. On that day, it was the most interesting meeting of my life. I have never seen something like that before and I don't think I'll ever see it again.

We had lunch in the hotel where we stay before home games. It's always the same waiters, the same familiar faces of the staff, whom I guess are chosen for being very discreet. There was one guy, though, I had never seen before, a waiter serving hot drinks. I didn't think much about it. He must have been a new guy.

In the final match-day meetings, we rarely sit down to watch any clips or look at a tactics board. Mikel is doing them very differently, in his own way. He will have us playing cards or little ball games to get those competitive juices flowing. He wants to switch us on, activate our minds. In the first part of that meeting, he laid out lots of cards on a big table. They had football terms like 'man on', 'set piece', 'win your duel' and so on written on them. He said, 'Okay guys, we need to start the game with winning your duel. Who's going to take that first card?' You had to pick it out before the other team at the other end of the table got there. It doesn't sound like much, but footballers are such a competitive lot, even a simple game like that becomes fiercely contested.

Then, for the second part, Mikel announced it was going to be another 'players vs staff freestyle battle'. The other day, it had been me against Nicolas 'Nico' Jover, our set-piece specialist, and I had won. So the manager says, 'It's rematch today. Alex, let's see if you can do it again.' So I get up and do a few tricks and so on. Then it's Nico's turn. But he's holding his hamstring, saying he's injured and can't play. Mikel looks around the room and says, 'We need a substitute. Anyone?' At that moment, that waiter raises his hand. Mikel says, 'Okay. You can try.' And guess what? This guy is killing it. He's basically destroying us. He even nutmegs Saka. Everyone's is looking at each other like, 'What the fuck is this?' Everyone's cheering him on and laughing.

Turns out he's a professional freestyler with millions of followers whom Mikel had planted at the hotel as a waiter. You realise how much work must have gone into that behind the scenes. That guy was there for at least three hours undercover, serving up coffee and cakes and waiting patiently for his big moment. The mood in the camp was incredible after that. People were buzzing on the way to the bus. That whole thing really pushed the right buttons. But it happens so often. Every one of Mikel's meetings is special.

Sometimes they can be physical, but they're more about getting in your head and setting the mood. We had one where every player was given a lemon, a knife and a glass. Mikel said, 'Guys, I want you to squeeze these lemons as hard as you can. In the end, we will add all of it in a bowl and we will see how much we can achieve together. The juice is our team magic.' Everyone starts cutting and squeezing. Then Mikel calls time. 'Let's see how much you squeezed.' He went to one of the players and said, 'Did you squeeze enough?' 'Yes, boss.' 'Okay, let me see.' He took the lemon, squeezed it and a bit of juice came out, still. 'Guys, this is the message,' he said, 'you can always add more. You can always give more.' Simple but quite effective.

Another one I really liked involved hundreds of big domino pieces. We came into the room and saw a ball next to a basket. There were very detailed instructions on what size dominos you could use and how they had to set up. Mikel asked us to work together and build this spiral of stones. 'Pay attention to the details and get all your angles right, because if only one stone is out of place, the whole thing breaks down,' he said.

Each one of us felt the responsibility. You don't want to be the one who lets the team down and have the chain reaction fail. The straight lines were easy but people working on the turns were nervous about getting it right. When we finally pushed the first domino, people were praying it would all run smoothly; they were super nervous. But the ball made it to the basket and the whole room blew up with relief and happiness. Again, a simple idea, but it worked so well to put everybody in good spirits before a big game and remind them that we were in this together. And that's the emotion you take into the game because everything else – the tactics, the line-ups, and so on – will have already been talked about well before.

Let's say the game is on Saturday, 3 p.m., and we have all week to prepare. In the two sessions on Monday and Tuesday, when it feels as if the game is still a long while away, we will focus on the basics. Honing our positional game, for example, or addressing our weaknesses. Sometimes, the coaches will just work with specific units, like the left side, and practise certain drills against the staff team or some youngsters. Sometimes, it can be the back four playing against the attackers. Everyone knows we're spending a lot of time on set pieces as well. We pay a lot of attention to throw-ins, free kicks and corners, and the work Nico and the team put in is really paying off.

Wednesday is rest day. Then Thursday and Friday are all about the next game and the next opponents. On Thursday, we might focus on our attacking game. What do we need to do when we have the ball, how do they defend, where are their weak spots and how do we best exploit them? Friday will then be more about the defensive side. We will practise either 11 vs 11 or against the Under-21s or Under-18s, who pretend they are our next opponent. Sometimes you get a vague idea what the line-up will look like from those exercises, but not always; Mikel will mix it up quite a lot and keep everyone on their toes.

Those sessions always start with meetings and video analysis. The boss explains how he wants us to play and then replicates those situations on the training ground. Those tactical meetings are a real joy and pleasure for me. It's tricky to say how Mikel and Pep differ from each other, experience aside, but they both have similar ideas and do an unbelievable job in terms of explaining the game and what they want to see on the pitch. Every session is a revelation. Having spent five years at City, I often feel as if I should know these things, but there's something new to learn every day. I remember Declan Rice coming up to me early in the 2023-24 season, and saying, 'Wow! What a meeting. I never had football explained to me like that before in my life. Football looks so simple when you follow this, this and that.' It's like Johan Cruyff said: 'Football is a simple game.' It's hard to play simple football, though, unless you have a manager who breaks the game down into little chunks and makes you understand what matters. Take one or two touches, in the right areas. Always scan for opponents and team-mates. That's essentially it.

Declan asked me, 'Bro, is it the same at City?' 'Yes, it's the same. I've seen it all before a hundred times.' I was half-joking. It's not the same, but the principles are very, very similar. The aim is to dominate the game in all areas of the pitch. You start from the build-up, making sure you play through the first line of pressure, then keep on playing through the middle and into the final thirds. You need to be on top of your opponents everywhere.

In terms of footballing philosophy and the brilliance of its execution, Mikel is the closest to Pep. That's the feeling I get from talking to other players about their coaches. I'm very interested how different managers see the game and am always picking other players' minds about the way they are getting coached. Eggs can't teach chickens, so this is only an educated guess from me, but I get the sense that

Mikel is on a similar level to Pep and might one day surpass him. Pep has simply been around a bit longer; he's seen everything a 1,000 times already. But that's really it. I also love the passion the boss exudes. He is a winner. And like all winners, he demands maximum intensity. 'Boys,' he likes to say, 'you must do everything full throttle. Football, partying, or in the bedroom with your wives: everything at full throttle.'

I consider myself one of the luckiest guys in the world to have been educated by these two superb football brains and their ideas since I was 19 years old, for basically my entire professional life. Every day, I feel like the new kid in school, learning new things.

Great managers such as them make players and teams better. It's often the little things that make a huge difference. There's a lot of individual coaching going on every single day. Sometimes Mikel will stop the play to point something out, but most of the time he will take you aside and talk through a couple of things he will have noticed: 'Just turn your body a bit more.' 'Open up your foot this way.' 'If the ball is on the other side of the pitch, look at the position of your team-mates and the opponents and position yourself a little deeper, to have more time on the ball to make the right decisions.' 'Don't be in the same line as the opponent, go between the lines.' He doesn't just say it, though; he will show it too, moving on the pitch. Imitation is the best way to learn. After a while, it becomes automatic, you don't even think about it any more. You absorb all this knowledge and it seeps into your bones.

On top of that, you will get regular video clips from the analysts. For outsiders, it's hard to believe the amount of work that goes into it at a top club like Arsenal. The analysts never sleep. Four guys will watch every training session and every game, then stay up all night to clip things together and send you stuff afterwards.

If the home game on Saturday kicks off later than 3 p.m., we don't stay overnight in the hotel but just meet in the morning. Otherwise, we have to report for duty at 8 p.m. on Friday night. We leave the cars at the training ground in Colney and drive to the hotel in the bus. There might be a meeting before dinner, but that's usually rare and mostly happens if the opponent is especially difficult to play against. Otherwise, the big pre-match meeting happens on Saturday morning. That's when you will know the line-up. Then we all go for a walk to catch some fresh air. The second and last meeting will then be about activation and the little games I mentioned before.

From my own experience, I knew that nothing short of a perfect season would be enough to take the title from City. Unfortunately, we ran into a little dodgy spell in February, however. An Everton team re-energised by their new manager, Sean Dyche, edged us out at Goodison Park. James Tarkowski scored the only goal with a header from a corner. We then only drew 1-1 with Brentford under controversial circumstances: two of their players made blocks in offside positions to become active, but the referee let their goal stand. A 3-1 home defeat against Man City showed us the scale of the challenge. But we recovered quickly to go on another unbeaten run and defended the top spot.

Something had also changed in the supporters' behaviour that season. They truly believed in us and stuck with us. Take the home game against Bournemouth on 4 March. It was a must-win game against a side fighting relegation. But things didn't quite click. We found ourselves 2-0 down with just over 30 minutes to go and didn't really know what was going on. I've been told that in the past, the crowd would have been very unhappy at that point. But on this day, their faith never wavered. They pushed us and pushed us until the last second; no one left early to beat the traffic. We scored one, then another. Seven minutes into injury time, everyone's still there, screaming for the ball to go into the net. When Eddie Nketiah smashed in a half-volley from just outside the box, the stadium shook from joy. I turned to the sea of limbs and people falling over each other, and I couldn't see even one empty space.

12

The Wrong Side of Poznan

February 2023 came with a very sad anniversary. The 1-0 win at Leicester marked one year since the start of the war in Ukraine. The day before, our captain, Martin Ødegaard, approached me and said that he, the boss and the team wanted me to wear the armband to show their support and turn a spotlight on the continued suffering in my country. I was very proud and grateful. Being captain for the day helped to bring attention to our fight for survival at a time when many in the West had become a little blasé about it. It meant a lot to me that my club still very much cared. 'Today we wanted to win for him, for his loved ones, and for all the Ukrainian people that have inspired the world with that fighting spirit and with the togetherness they showed as a country,' Mikel said. 'If we can add some happiness today to them and reflecting on who Alex is for us, it was a good opportunity, so I'm delighted to dedicate that win to them.'

In April, we unfortunately dropped four points after being 2-0 up, against both West Ham (2-2) and Liverpool (2-2), before drawing a third game in a row, 3-3 at Southampton. We still controlled our own destiny going into the showdown at the Etihad five points clear of City, but they had two games in hand and an excellent recent record against us. Pep's side had beaten Arsenal on the last seven occasions. What could have been a decisive blow in the title race instead turned into a nightmare. Kevin De Bruyne galloped through midfield and dispatched a low shot into the corner to score after only seven minutes. We never settled. A header from John Stones, ruled onside after intervention from VAR, and another sublime finish from KDB, put the game to bed with less than an hour gone.

The crowd turned their backs to us, locked arms and did the 'Poznań' dance, jumping up and down. I had seen it countless times before at the Etihad but never as an opposition player. I struggle to put into words how bad I felt at that moment. The game was clearly over at that point, and they paid us zero respect by looking the other way, as if we weren't worthy of their attention. That, combined with the way City had swatted us away like some annoying little fly, made me ashamed and angry in equal measure. You feel absolutely powerless in that moment. You want to pick up the ball, dribble past seven players and score to respond to the crowd, but sadly, you can't do that. There was obviously nothing wrong with their celebrations; I would have joined in myself as a City fan. I really love and respect their fans for all the support they have shown me during my time there. But that didn't make me feel any better. In 27 years of my life, I had never been this embarrassed before. It truly was the worst moment of my career.

That devastating 4-1 defeat put City in total control of the title race. We were still top but could only hope and pray they would somehow slip up in the last few games. Deep down, I knew there was not much chance of that. Not with City. In a position like that, they were unstoppable. They just control the variables better than anyone else.

Space and time work differently in the Premier League. You have so much less of it than anywhere else. I might be wrong, but I'm pretty certain this is the best league in the world. What makes it special is that you can't switch off, not even for a second. The game against Chelsea brought that home to me in a painful manner. Smart people try to learn from other people's mistakes. But sometimes you have to be right in the thick of it yourself to fully understand what's going on.

We were 3-0 up. The game was essentially over. Chelsea were trying to make the scoreline a bit more respectable and we were trying to score more goals, so the game was bit too open, quite up and down. There were many spaces between the lines. We weren't very compact. These things can happen when the gap between midfielders and defenders starts getting too wide as legs and minds tire.

We kept on going forwards regardless and I was blowing a bit. We lose the ball. I'm running back to recover, just as coaches the world over have drilled it into kids since time eternal. Bust your guts getting back in position, then take a rest there. That's what I did. I was about to take a deep breather, and for a split second lost the winger on my blind side. Normally, your job as a full-back is to look at three things at the same time. First, where is the ball? Second, where is your centre-back, because you need to keep the line. Third, where is your winger? I watched the first two but lost track of my opponent, Noni Madueke. He made a run behind me. By the time I spotted him, he was already past me, latching on to a perfectly weighted ball from Mateo Kovačić. Bang. 3-1. I thought to myself, 'Damn, this league is unbelievable.' One moment is all it takes for someone to punch in you in the face. Even a team that's already been beaten and should have given up the ghost.

Any side in the Premier League can do this to you. A few minutes later, I was subbed. The boss had planned to take me off for a while, it had nothing to do with us conceding, but I was sick to my stomach. He shook my hand and I said, 'Mister, I'm sorry, I just lost focus for a second.' He said something like, 'We'll speak about it later,' but it wasn't necessary. I knew I had messed up.

In these moments, it's important not to become despondent and to keep a sense of perspective. Coming home to your family often does the trick. After a bad day in the office, you get in the door, your daughter gives you a hug, and you simply forget about anything else in this world. There's no better feeling. I didn't notice it straight away, but becoming a father has changed my outlook on life. Before Eva was born in August 2021, I did quite a few crazy things. I jumped out of a plane once with a parachute, for example. I had lots of energy and felt very brave. Now I have less energy – two toddlers will do that to you – and I'm much more responsible. I think of them first. I can't do anything that puts them in danger. If I'm gone because my parachute doesn't open or the plane goes down, they will grow up without a dad. I can't take that risk, however small.

Other dads think I'm the star, coming home to three amazing girls every day. It doesn't feel like that. Not yet, anyway. I think I rank lower than Louie and Mia, our two French bulldogs, in the household.

Louie came to us first. For over a year, Vlada had nagged me about getting a puppy. She was on a mission. So one day, I went to a breeder. He showed me two beautiful puppies, brother and sister. The girl had these beautiful blue eyes and I thought about taking her but then I went for the boy in the end: Louie.

Vlada was so happy. Mission accomplished. But then two months later, Louie needed injections. The breeder went to the vet with us and brought Louie's mum with him for comfort. Then we went for a coffee at his place, just around the corner. There were half a dozen more puppies there and they all crowded around Louie and licked him. One dog in particular was all over him. It was the girl I had originally chosen. They just couldn't be separated. And so we went home with two dogs. We thought it would be easier if they had each other. But toilet training them was pretty difficult. We lived in a flat at the time. Every morning, I got up to clean the mess they had made. I thought it was impossible for two little dogs to produce so much stuff. I took some videos because I thought no one would believe me. Now that we live in north London with its many green spaces, it's a little easier. Trouble is, the vet has put them on a special diet which makes them fart non-stop. I will spare you the details but, suffice to say, I've had guests pass out in the living room a couple of times.

Quality time with the family aside, it's also important that you switch off from time to time, that you can clear your mind, and know exactly what helps you find a bit of peace. For some players, it's golf, sex or PlayStation. For me, it's playing *Counter-Strike*, a first-person shooter game. When I play with my friends, I'm in another world. I can get rid of all the tension and negativity. And then when I'm back in real life, I feel brand-new.

Counter-Strike is a big passion of mine. It was a dream to get involved, which is why I founded a professional team called Passion UA in 2023. They're made up of young kids from Ukraine and a coach who used to manage one of the country's best sides, Na'Vi. He's called Mykhailo Blahin, nickname: Kane. But, unlike his football namesake, he has won big trophies, including a couple of World Cups.

It's five players and a coach, a proper sport. They are professionals. They train for about eight hours a day, go to the gym and on walks together, do strategy meetings. There are a lot of tactics involved, you don't just go out and shoot at people. Three to four times a year, they do boot camps, too. We started from the bottom, playing small competitions, but they've been very good so far. They nearly qualified for the World Cup after only eight months together. We didn't expect that; we thought it might take them two years to be at this level, as teams who make the World Cup can earn millions of dollars. During Covid, audience numbers and prize money went through the roof.

But being in Ukraine, they also face challenges. For starters, everyone's worried they might have to serve in the army and go to war. So far, they've taken only men over 25, but maybe that will change. They also have connectivity issues. One of our guys couldn't get a decent line for a game against Bleed, one of the elite teams in Ukraine. My business partner Arti (Aretmijs Rjabovs), who helped set up the team, called me and said, 'We need help.' They made a late substitution: I stepped in.

Counter-Strike is played in three sets, called maps. They had lost the first one, without me. We were 3-10 down in the second one but managed to win 16-12. In the decisive map, we narrowly lost 13-11. Still, social media went nuts because I played under my real name. Bleed's owner was not at all happy that a footballer managed to win one set against his highly trained outfit. In an interview, he threatened to change half the team.

At the moment, Passion UA is perhaps the third best team in Ukraine, in terms of organisation and quality. The first one is called Na'Vi, but they've been here for years. They have a player who's like the Messi of *Counter-Strike*. He makes millions. A team from Saudi took him on a month's loan and apparently paid him a million dollars. Crazy stuff. But at this level, it's serious business. I only play with my friends for fun but not much. It's impossible to find the time with two young kids. But when they're away or in kindergarten, I can relax a bit in front of the screen.

It's important to clear your mind from football at times. Some might think a professional footballer's life is so easy. And of course it is, compared with many other jobs. But the pressure here in the Premier League is at another level. This is the highest level of football you can play at. The pace, the calendar, the expectation from supporters, the competition. If you can't be at your best every three days, you will fail. I'm sure it's a similar story in Spain or Germany or Italy or France. I have never played there. Similar, but not the same. Watching the games, I can see the difference in terms of pace. It's not a secret. I'm not the first one to tell you that. With all due respect to the other leagues, the quality is the highest here. Look at the players that are coming here from all over the world. Someone with a big price tag, where will he go? To one or two Spanish clubs, to Bayern Munich, perhaps. Everyone else is going to England.

The trick is to remember what an amazing privilege it is to play here. You can't be all bad if you're playing in this league, you must be worth something. Take heart from that. If you couldn't do it, you wouldn't be here. That's step one. Step two: enjoy it. You were dreaming about these moments as a kid. Millions of boys and girls would love to be in your position. Think about the pleasure you get from kicking a ball around.

I once saw that Pablo Picasso said, 'It took me a lifetime to draw like a child.' Don't take that long as a professional footballer to find the child inside you again. Never forget how much you've loved playing football as a little boy, and how much that little boy would give if you told him he'd be a professional footballer one day. I don't think you can be the best version of yourself unless you're enjoying what you're doing. You have to enjoy it. It's a pleasure to play football, a dream. I've seen some guys turn up in the morning at the training ground, play football, and go home again, with no emotional involvement at all. They're just putting a shift in, as if they were going to the office. Then they go home and they don't really care. I'm not saying they were playing badly, not at all. But I can't relate to that attitude.

In 2010, I read an interview with French defender Benoît Assou-Ekotto. He said: 'I don't know why everyone lies. I play football for the money. It's my job, not my passion.' I was very young and really didn't understand that attitude at the time. Actually, I still don't understand it today. To me, football is happiness, a dream. I could never see it as just a job; I love the game far too much. Maybe he didn't enjoy it because he played for Tottenham Hotspur? That can't be a lot of fun.

If you do a job – any job, not just football – that you're not enjoying, you're in the wrong place. Unless you don't have any other options, of course. I realise that not everyone's in a position to pick and choose. But if you do have other possibilities that bring you more satisfaction, take them. I think a lot about that when I have played a bad game or made a mistake and spend too much attention and energy on it. After a while, I tell myself, why do this? Don't waste your time worrying about things that have already happened. That's gone now. Analyse it, learn from it, move on. But don't beat yourself up too much. It's gone, it's happened already. If you think too much about it and are too hard on yourself, you can start to kill your own confidence. That must not happen.

Football is life, so we need to live it, because time flies.

Maybe those who treat the game as a mere job have the right idea and I'm wrong, taking things to heart too much. But I can't do it differently. I cannot come in, shake everyone's hand without a smile and a joke or two, kick a ball around and then leave again. For me, that's soul-destroying. You need to enjoy each other's company. You need to laugh together. Laughter brings you closer together.

Of course, the timing needs to be right. You can't be a clown. And you need to know who you're dealing with. Humour is very individual. I had this running joke with Reiss Nelson that there was no limit to his bad fashion sense, because his clobber got worse and worse every day. People were in stitches, nearly crying from laughter in the dressing room. My former team-mates at City might not believe me when they read this, as they used to wind me up non-stop about my clothes. But not everyone has the same sense of humour. With Takehiro Tomiyasu, you can joke all day and the most you'll get out of him is a wry smile in the evening. And you don't know – did he find that funny or not?

I'm not the only one at Arsenal, though. There are some players who are constantly on the wind-up. A favourite prank of theirs is to hide people's phones. They love to target me, but I'm outsmarting them by hiding it myself. I've also been thrown into the ice bath a few times. But that's good. I love that. Those kind of moments bring you closer as a team, as a family, and they spill over onto the pitch. When it's your brother next to you, you fight harder for each other.

When you do things as a team, in unison, even hard work turns into fun. Remember what Pep said about his Barcelona running like animals? They could do so because all of them did it. It's not a slog, it can be pure joy, especially if all that running helps you to dominate games with the ball. To have this much fun, you need to work hard. Then you don't even feel it.

Finishing second and getting back into the Champions League for the first time in six years was a huge achievement for this team. We had given the supporters a lot of joy and hope. We had proved to ourselves and everyone else that we could compete against the best side in Europe and push them all the way. And we had made going to the Emirates a fun experience again. Teams were scared to go there. So it wasn't all bad. But in the end, we had also let down our fans by losing momentum in the league.

However awful they felt about us coming short, it was ten times worse for us as players. You know how much it means to everybody at the club, and to disappoint your supporters is terrible.

Some pundits were quick to accuse us of bottling it. I've always found that phrase and the idea behind it a bit weird. It implies that those who come second lack the moral fibre of the winners, that they're somehow cowards. Maybe that's true in some isolated cases but it certainly wasn't for us. Without a strong mentality and the courage to play very intricate attacking football, a young team that had been nowhere near the title race in nearly a decade could never have pushed City this hard.

Gary Neville said that our fault was to 'over-celebrate' wins. He mentioned me shouting out to Arsenal fans out of my car window after a home win against Aston Villa. Yes, I accept the blame. I would have never done it if I had known it would cost us winning the league two months later. But seriously. I've done it quite a few times passing the Tollington pub on my way back home. I love that spot. It's always packed with Gooners, and I love sharing my happy emotions with them when we've won. There's always a great energy after a good result at the Emirates, because winning Premier League matches is quite hard.

But I don't mind Gary Neville or the other TV pundits having a go. In fact, I love it. I used to watch him, Jamie Carragher, Rio Ferdinand and all the other legends as a little kid and now they're talking about me? Amazing. I must have done something right in my life. Please continue to talk about me as much as you can. I absolutely love it. Good or bad, I love to listen and learn from their opinions.

Bottlers? I think the real explanation was a little less esoteric. One, we got unlucky with injuries. Losing William Saliba at the back was a huge problem, even though we had a very good squad. Two, City simply had vastly more experience than us. They know, having done it so many times before, that every single game is important if you want to win the title. You cannot just focus on the big games.

Here's an example of what I mean: that home game against Southampton. A routine affair. Or so it should have been. Some of our thoughts had already turned forwards to the big top-of-the-table clash. But you won't get away with that. That's impossible in this league. We started poorly, went 2-0 down and only managed to get a point when the final whistle went. Beating them would have given us a lot more confidence, the three points aside. But we took our eyes off the ball, just a little, and barely came away with a 3-3 draw that slowed our momentum and put wind in City's sails.

Three, we lost three head-to-heads against them that season, including two defeats in the league. Two draws would have been enough for us to finish ahead of them. That's how close we got. But they were still a little better than us, we had to admit that. From the front to the back, they are a machine, built over many years. Take Ederson, the goalkeeper. He's like an extra outfield player for them. The confidence he has on the ball is ridiculous. He knows what he needs to do with the ball. He knows there is always going to be someone in the middle, ready to receive the ball, or to move into space as the third man with the right timing. These guys have been playing these patterns forever. For us it was year one, with a really young team. But it takes time to build a winning side. Even Pep, with all his previous successes elsewhere, had to learn that in the Premier League.

13

United for Ukraine

I went back to Ukraine for the first time in two years in the summer of 2023, travelling by plane to Chișinău in Moldova, and then eight hours by car. It was a strange feeling. I was so happy to be back in the country I was born and raised in for a few days, to be back in my homeland, but I also felt so much pain. It was a completely different experience seeing all this destruction with my own eyes, rather than on TV or on my smartphone.

Andriy Shevchenko and I met President Volodymyr Zelensky in Kyiv. We spoke about our work with United24, an organisation that raises money and tries to make a difference on the ground. They collect money to rebuild damaged infrastructure, buy drones for the military, ambulances for the health system. They look after dozens and dozens of similar projects. He was really happy to see us and hear about our plans. United24 connects Ukrainians abroad in their efforts to help the country. There's not a single Ukrainian who hasn't been touched one way or the other by this war. All of us are in the same team. We need to try to make the best out of this horrible situation.

When I went into his office, I was surprised by how people around him were working. It was a very friendly atmosphere and it was very easy to talk to him. I said to him, 'Mr President, I know this isn't part of the script, but these words come from somewhere deep inside my heart: we are so happy that we have you as our president. All my family and friends feel the same. I don't know what would happen to our country if you weren't there.'

I hadn't told anyone in advance that I would say these words to him because I wasn't sure if it was appropriate. They had tried to prepare me – 'Don't be scared. Don't shake' – stuff like that. No one told me what I could or couldn't say, but I had prepared myself mentally – I didn't want to get too emotional. But then I shook his hand, started to speak and I felt very comfortable and close to him.

When you look deep into his eyes, you see how tough it is for him, how much pressure he is under. He looks like a completely different person compared with how he was three years ago. He's aged so much from the stress and pressure, it's scary. I was wondering what it feels like to sit in his chair and live his life, just for one second. I'm not sure I could do it. I don't think I could shoulder the responsibility for millions of people, knowing my family and I are the number one target to be killed. It must be hard to live like that.

The night of the invasion, he received a call from the US president telling him the Russians were trying to assassinate him and his family. He was offered an airlift to safety and he replied, 'Listen, I really appreciate everything you're doing. But I don't need a taxi. I need guns and bullets.' Talk about an inspirational leader.

A few years ago, he was a TV actor. Isn't that incredible? But his story just goes to show that it doesn't matter what you have done in the past. What's important is who you are today and what you are doing now. I have no words for the job he is doing for our country.

I don't understand politics. But meeting him, I realised he is absolutely our hero. He is our leader and the man whom you want to follow through these dark days. We are very lucky to have him. He's a brave man who's showed the whole world we will not be cowed by terrorist aggression. We will resist.

We were driving for many hours each day with the United24 staff, going past shattered houses. There were hundreds, thousands of homes that used to be alive with families, filled with love and happiness, blown up or burned down one day by terrorists for no reason.

There is something about being a father that makes it all even more unbearable. Your mind is flooded by some very dark thoughts; you begin to imagine what it must feel like to lose your home, to lose your livelihood, to lose someone you love. But the more you see of all this senseless death, the less you really understand it. What are these people trying to achieve by dropping bombs on us, ruining ordinary people's lives? All they were doing was working all day to pay the rent or the mortgage for those houses. And within one second it was all rubble, and entire families were gone. Why? And where do those who survived go from there?

Our nanny in London is from Ukraine. She used to live in a region that is now occupied by Russia, with her husband and two teenage daughters, aged 14 and 16. They came to her city, looted the houses, killed and raped. She managed to escape with the two girls, but all they could take were three backpacks. That's all that's left from their former life. It was a good, normal life. The father left for another city, which was still under control of Ukraine. He's not allowed to leave the country, so they haven't seen each other for more than two years now. This is just one story but there are millions of them, and many of these stories are much worse.

Russia wants more territory, I understand that. But I don't understand why. Look how big they are. It's the only place in Europe where you can drive for three hours and not see a single soul around you. It's a country rich with natural resources, yet millions and millions of Russians, perhaps as many as one quarter of the population, still use outhouse toilets. Almost 70 per cent of them have never been abroad. They have two passports: one for identification, one for travelling. But more than two-thirds of their people don't have that second passport. They don't know about Europe and our life here. They're being told all the West is trying to destroy Russia.

Instead of bettering the lives of their people, they spend billions on bombs and rockets wrecking Ukraine. They could use this money to build on all that empty ground. They could make it a new Dubai, inviting people to live there and invest. They could be the most powerful country in the world. But no. They go out to destroy their neighbours' country and kill hundreds of thousands of people on both sides for land they don't need. Their grandsons and granddaughters are still going to pay for the rebuild of all those Ukrainian houses and facilities for decades to come because of sanctions.

We went to see the Mykhailo-Kotsyubinsky Lyceum, a destroyed school we are rebuilding as part of the United24 initiative, two and a half hours north of Kyiv. It's a big school that took in kids from ten villages from the surrounding areas. In the Chernihiv region of Ukraine, the terrorists bombed a lot of places and invaded when the war started. They were heading for Kyiv, trying to take the capital and kill our president. One of the cleaners was killed by a missile, but it could have been so much worse: 100 people, including some babies, were sheltering in the basement.

Russian soldiers stole the 30 pieces of bread the headmaster had prepared for the people sleeping there. He also told us that many former graduates died on the battlefield. He was worn down by grief but at the same time totally committed to rebuilding his pupils' lives.

I met some children who told me what went on when masked soldiers came to their homes, took away everything of value and committed atrocities too dreadful to repeat here. Some lost their parents. Some relayed their stories without emotion, as if those horrors had befallen someone else. Some had no words, only tears. They don't understand why these things happened to them. It was heartbreaking. You know those kids weren't lying. They can't lie. They don't know how to. We kicked a ball around on a pitch that was partially destroyed. It was a moment of normality and happiness in a place where hope has been in short supply. Even the air smelt different there. I can't describe it.

For most of the trip, I was in shock and crying. Everyone we met had a story but not everyone could tell it. Some were too scared; they wanted to keep those memories buried. How do you carry on with your life if you or someone from your family has been raped, if your children or parents were killed? Imagine you are one of the parents of the 20,000 kids forcibly taken to Russia. That is one of the most painful parts for me. Imagine being at home, looking at their empty bedroom every day, at the empty chair in the kitchen, and wondering what they are doing to them. They are teaching them to be Russian. They want to erase our Ukrainian identity.

I'm not an expert in human rights and international law. But what do you call the attempt to destroy an entire country, to destroy our culture, our infrastructure? People were freezing to death because they knocked out the power stations in the winter of 2022-23. Many didn't have enough to eat. The aim here is clearly to kill as many people as possible. If that's not genocide, it can't be far off.

The people at United24 work incredibly hard, 24 hours a day, like the name suggests. They drive all round the country from 6 a.m. until late at night each day, seeing people, raising money. I spent a day with them. They sleep in tiny rooms with bunk beds, get up at the crack of dawn to go to another of those places where death has visited.

They don't have nearly enough people or resources to deal with this nightmare. There are hundreds of schools that need rebuilding, millions of people who need help. They have raised lots of money but are still barely scratching the surface. They keep on going anyway. There are no more than ten people, always on their phones and laptops, talking non-stop to those who might be able to help or raise money. I think sometimes they forget to eat. We went to a little roadside restaurant on the way to the school. One of them, a young woman, was working on her laptop, and they asked her what she wanted to order. 'Anything,' she said, 'just get me anything.' We ordered something for her, they brought her plate, but when we left I saw she hadn't even touched it.

We need about a million euros to rebuild the school and have raised most of it. It's just one school out of hundreds, in one place, out of thousands. But it's not nothing. These kids have been scarred for life. It's terrifying to think about it. But by giving them a school to go back to, we can at least bring back a bit of normality. We owe it to them to take the war out of their lives. They are our future.

I often think of a story my aunt has told me. She works as a kindergarten teacher in my home town. One day, she was playing with the kids outside. Suddenly, there was a Ukrainian plane above them in the sky. It was very loud. The kids started to scream. They fell to the floor, shaking with fear. They thought the plane might drop a bomb on them. I see this image in my mind and I just want to cry. I feel so sorry for them. They were born in Covid times, and now they're living through a war, and their life is bombs, drones, sirens, almost every day.

Some of the volunteers I talked to had other horrible stories. When the Nova Kakhovka dam burst in June 2023 — most people think the Russians did it to stop the Ukrainian counter-offensive — a lot of people weren't able to leave their houses in time. Some were too old. I was told about one woman who stood on her roof, with two babies in her arms, born just a few months earlier. She was hanging on, trying to survive. But they couldn't get her. They all died.

Afterwards, I came back to Kyiv and heard my first siren. It was the middle of the night, about 2.30 a.m. They usually send the rockets and drones while everyone is sleeping, to maximise the terror. My wife, her brother and I were all sleeping in the apartment. Suddenly there was this howling sound, like the noise from a horror movie. It was so loud. I woke up but was so tired. I had driven for many hours that day. My wife wanted to go to the underground parking lot to hide, but I said, 'Listen, honestly, I'm so tired, I can't go. I just want to stay here in bed.' They both went to the window to see what was going on in the sky.

And just above the house, our air defence systems were shooting down the drones and missiles. There were so many big bangs. I was too tired to get out of bed but I heard the explosions. My mind went to the parents trying to comfort their kids in these moments. How are you putting your little ones to bed and comforting them when the sirens are blaring and there are missiles heading your way? The whole city was on its feet, worried the bombs would fall on them. It's so sad to think that children have had to live like that for over two years now, with no end in sight.

In Kyiv, people are just trying to live their lives. There are still a lot of cars in the city centre, there's even a bit of traffic at times. It's good; it shows that we're still alive. But it's a city in war mode. There's a curfew before midnight. No one is allowed out after that. Police and security services are roaming the streets, trying to catch spies and saboteurs working for the other side. If you're visiting friends in the evening, you have to leave early to make sure you're in bed before the curfew. Otherwise, the police will ask questions, arrest you and take you to the police station for an interrogation.

People are so tired of being scared all the time. I have friends who tell me, 'We cannot just live in distress. We need to carry on. We need to earn money. We need to work. We need to feed our kids, our families.' They're just trying to carry on as normal, as much as they can. But unfortunately, there's someone dying every day – soldiers on the battlefront, or civilians in their beds, when their homes get destroyed. I just don't know when this war is going to end.

Sometimes when you are in that mood, you're just trying to visualise and remember the lives we lived before all that. When we could go out without a curfew and could fly direct from Kyiv to London or anywhere else in Europe. We were able to make plans. Young people were able to dream. Now, boys older than 18 can't leave the country because of conscription and they can't work properly either, because that draft letter might come through the door any day. Everything is on hold while we fight for survival. This really is the toughest period for our country and our people.

It was Andriy Shevchenko's idea to stage Game4Ukraine, a charity match and concert at Stamford Bridge to raise money for the rebuilding of the school and to send a powerful message to the world that we're sticking together. Nine months of work went into it; it was so hard to sign all the agreements. In the UK, people rarely say yes or no to you. They will avoid giving you a straight answer. It can take weeks, if not months, before you get a response one way or the other. We were very worried we might not be able to pull it off. More than that, we were really nervous. Would we sell enough tickets? We didn't want TV channels in the UK and in Ukraine showing an empty stadium. That would have been very bad. It was all extremely stressful for us.

I remember match day, when I arrived at the hotel where the legends and celebrities were staying. I saw all these famous faces and finally believed it was truly happening. All that tension turned into relief and joy. Of course it was raining that day – that's London in August for you – but even with the poor weather, the stadium was almost full, as more than 30,000 came. It was all worth it. Not just for the money we raised for the school. We also showed everyone coming together and making a stand for Ukraine.

I nearly cried when the Ukrainian and the British national anthems were played and everyone stood arm in arm for a minute's silence afterwards. We also listened to a very heartfelt video message from President Zelensky, who thanked everyone for their support. I could only play 11 minutes for 'Team Zinchenko' against Sheva's side as I wasn't fully fit, but sharing the pitch with these big names was so much fun and a true honour. Gerard Piqué, Fabio Cannavaro, Jens Lehmann, Petr Čech, William Gallas, Joe Cole, Per Mertesacker, with Arsène Wenger and Emma Hayes managing on the touchline... Amazing.

I had also invited Thierry Henry, the best Arsenal player of all time, to play. 'I'm not sure it's a good idea. With my pace, you'll have to run for two players playing against me,' he joked. I said, 'Listen, with my pace, I've got no chance against you anyway. You're much quicker even now!' Unfortunately he couldn't join us in the end, but he really wanted to play.

Before the game, I came up to Clarence Seedorf and said, 'Before I shake your hand, I always had a dream of touching your quads. Do you mind?' He was laughing his head off. But I had to do it, at least once. Have you ever seen his quads? They are an absolute joke. And my god, he was so good. Still. He scored an unbelievable goal, 'chopping' the ball from one side to confuse his opponent and scoring with his left foot from outside the box. Such quality. And he played the full 90 minutes. He and Robert Pires. It's crazy how fit they both were. Pires, at 50, was so sharp on the pitch as well. You can smell and feel his quality. What a player.

Staging this game sent a very powerful message: it showed people back home that we are not alone. For me, it was one of the proudest moments in my life. It was a dream come true. Football doesn't always mix well with politics. People want to escape their worries when they are going to the stadium. They don't want to be reminded of everything that's wrong in the world. There are also commercial factors at play. A few clubs in the Premier League were initially afraid to take a strong stance against the war, but by and large, the reaction has been great. Russian teams were quickly banned from competitions and football has sent a strong message that it will not close its eyes to one country trying to eradicate another one. As much as people like to criticise our sport for being out of touch and too obsessed with money, football has largely taken the right stance on this.

I sometimes get asked if I feel guilty about not being in Ukraine. I have thought a lot about that. The question is, where can I be more helpful for my country? Fighting as a soldier, or playing football in the Premier League, earning some money I can send to people, to the army, using my platform to speak out and trying to tell the rest of the world what is going on there?

I'm not saying that I'm the voice for Ukraine. I would never claim to be that. I'm certainly no hero, either. Far from it. There's nothing heroic at all about playing football in England and speaking to the media while our brave soldiers battle on the frontlines and people back home live under constant fear. But if, let's say, 100 people are sitting in a press conference room and ten of them are paying attention to what I'm saying, I feel I have done something good and positive. And these ten people can spread the information. These ten people can tell our stories to someone else. And then others will know others who can spread the message and join in, as much as they can. I am proud that I am able to contribute a little bit to the rebuilding of our country and help those who work tirelessly on the ground.

14

Chasing Perfection

Trent Alexander-Arnold is shaping up to strike the ball deep in his own half and I know what he's trying to do with my eyes closed: he will play Mohamed Salah in off my left shoulder. It's a classic Liverpool move against any team with a high defensive line. He or Virgil van Dijk can put the ball on a plate for Salah if there's no pressure on them. There's a bit of pressure from Gabi Jesus, but it's still a perfect ball. I'm turning towards goal as I run backwards, catching up with Salah. Attackers always have a head start in these situations: they can pick up speeding running forward while defenders have to react after holding the line.

He picks up the ball and starts running at me. If you're lucky, your centre-back is close enough to come over and help out. He can cover the inside and you the outside. It takes a split second to realise I'm on my own out there, but that split second is already too long. Salah, with one quick shuffle, has turned past me and fired a shot past David Raya. It's Liverpool's equaliser. We had led 1-0 at Anfield until that moment and played a brilliant game.

What I should have done, of course, is to prioritise the right things. Protect the inside. Close down his left foot. That's the most important thing. Make him cross with his weaker right foot, or shoot with it from a bad angle. The problem isn't that you don't know what to do, it's to do it quickly enough. I didn't. By the time I understood how I needed to position my body correctly in that moment, Raya was already picking the ball out of the net.

A 1-1 draw at Anfield is no disgrace. Coupled with a 1-0 win at home over Manchester City two months earlier, in October, it showed that we had taken another step forward as a team and had an even better chance of winning the Premier League. But I was really annoyed with myself for making the mistake that led to Liverpool's goal. We spoke about it in the dressing room, but I already knew what I had done wrong. I have watched that clip many, many times. Friends and people close to me, who know that I take these errors in my game very much to heart, attempted to console me afterwards: 'Bro, he's Mohamed Salah, he's one of the best wingers in the world. He does it every three days to every full-back in the world ...'. But that's a weak excuse. In fact, it's no excuse. It hurts me even more to hear this. I know he's one of the best, but I also know I could have still prevented this goal. I just had to do the right thing. Two steps to my right and the situation would have changed completely.

You have to draw the right lessons from these moments; make sure you react differently the next time this happens. That's why the game doesn't finish with the final whistle for me. I go over the 90 minutes in my head and analyse how it measured against the points on my personal checklist. What did I do well? What did I do wrong? What did I let my opponent do? Did I defend well? How much did I bring to the table in attack? How many sharp passes, good crosses, good deliveries did I provide? How much did I create for the team?

Sometimes I watch clips of myself in the early years at Man City on YouTube, just to look at the difference to how I'm playing now, and I get angry. Sure, there were mitigating circumstances. I was a young player in a new position. But seriously: how can you be so boring, passing it sideways and back all the time? I played a game like that for Arsenal and actually wanted to throw up afterwards, I was so disgusted with myself. Not a single line-breaking pass, nothing special at all. It's not good enough.

I'd like to think I'm quite honest with myself. I've got a pretty good idea how the game went for me. I also get a strong sense by looking at Vlada after the game. If she wants to talk to me, I've done okay. If she doesn't want to talk to me, I've been rubbish. She either wants to leave me alone out of pity, because she knows I'm hard on myself, or because she's embarrassed. Maybe a bit of both.

Thirdly, there are the numbers. Arsenal put the game stats on screen in the dressing room the day after a game. It's the information from the GPS vests, sprints, fastest pace and overall distance covered. I never look at pace because I already know I'm not the fastest player on the pitch. I have different qualities. But I will compare the distance I've run to the other full-back. That screen is a subtle motivational tool, because everyone looks at it. You don't want to be the player who runs the least. Some players ask the analytics people for stats on passing accuracy and so on. Arsenal have all the data. But for me, the priority is always the team, not individual numbers. The results are what truly matters, not how much you've run. You need to win.

And win we did, even if we didn't quite dominate games as much as we had done in the previous season. The added workload of playing in the Champions League made a difference, and it also takes time for new players to bed in and for everything to click. The more intricate the system, the more time it takes. And it doesn't get more intricate than Arteta's vision of the game.

It would be easy to go out and play football 'the old way', line up in a basic 4-4-2 or 4-3-3 or whatever, sit in your own half when the opponent has the ball, go for it with your attacking players once you win the ball and leave the defenders behind for protection. Easy, in terms of understanding the game plan. But against the best teams in the world – many of whom happen to play in the Premier League – you will suffer if you don't have a detailed plan, as they do everything as a unit. You'll be constantly outnumbered in certain areas and chasing shadows.

To play like Arsenal is much harder, in the sense that it's more complicated. We press collectively in certain patterns and set specific traps for every game. During the summer, I saw rumours about big players joining us. I tried to visualise them playing in our team and, with some of them, I just couldn't see it. I don't think they could cope, because everyone runs like an animal here, in each position. That's so important for any top team. If only one player doesn't do it, you're in big trouble.

On the ball, there are lots of moves and principles you need to adhere to. You can't just freestyle. There are so many things to take into account; it's like learning a new language. It doesn't happen overnight, no matter how talented you are. Don't underestimate the challenge of coming into a team that's already been together for a while with a defined identity and players who know each other inside out.

In those early months of the 2023-24 season, there was a lot of attention on Kai Havertz, our new signing from Chelsea. Some people said he was struggling because they were looking at the price tag, at his goals and assists, and demanded more. But there's a media view and then there's the view from the inside, which is often completely different. Watching him in training every day, I can tell you we didn't think he was struggling at all. Forget the goals and the assists, he was working so hard. It was immediately clear he would be an important player for Arsenal, because of his skills and ability to play in a variety of positions. We didn't have a player who combines so many top attributes before. He understands the game well. He can fight for the ball because he's so tall. He can keep the ball because he's technically strong. He has amazing timing to run into the box, can finish, and he was improving every single game.

I love Kai's runs. You can trust his timing, it's so precise. Even if it doesn't come off because the player on the ball opts for a different pass, he's dragged one or two defenders with him. Take the first goal in our 3-1 win over Liverpool in February 2024. I moved the ball into the centre from the left near the halfway line and saw Martin Ødegaard had a bit of space. Before I passed the ball, Kai had already started to make his run into the space van Dijk had left to attack Ødegaard. A beautiful first-time ball from him put Kai through, one-on-one with the keeper, and Bukayo scored from the rebound.

Having a player like that in your ranks is a tremendous asset. Kai will improve your team's game in a very selfless manner, knowing quite a lot of people won't get what he's doing as it happens 'off-camera' while they are just looking at the ball. They will scream for numbers, they want big moments, whereas 100 good moments per game are far more valuable for a team who want to dominate. Kai was ready for that pressure, and he was doing an amazing job for us.

Another newcomer also impressed me a lot. I knew Declan Rice was an amazing player from his time at West Ham, but the consistency he showed in games for Arsenal was a real credit to him. He's a fantastic guy. From the first day, you could see he was a leader, on and off the pitch.

Up until that Liverpool draw on 23 December, we had lost only two games in the league: narrow 1-0 defeats at Newcastle United and Aston Villa. Key moments went against us in both matches, controversially so in the case of the defeat at St James' Park, and it was the same story in our first home defeat, 2-0 against West Ham, five days after the Liverpool draw. We went through a little slump in that busy period, losing 2-1 at Fulham and 2-0 at home to Liverpool in the FA Cup. But the underlying data showed there was nothing substantially wrong with our game. Nobody panicked.

Still, a break in Dubai came at the right time for us. Arsenal organised the trip so we could take our families and had plenty of time off. It was a nice blend of work on the training ground and bonding with team-mates. There was a barbecue for everyone, we all got to know each other better and came away with a closer connection to each other. Extra time to practise the little things that can get lost when you play every three days was also a huge boost. We worked very hard on set pieces with our specialist coach, Nico. You can have an excellent game, but one moment of bad organisation from a corner or free kick can kill you. At the same time, one good set piece can help you make the breakthrough when you're struggling to create openings from open play. Those small details can take on an outsized importance when games are tight.

The difference Nico has made since coming over from City in 2021 is unreal. I'm a great believer in the idea that someone working really hard will always be rewarded.

That is Nico summed up. We scored 22 goals from set pieces in the league last season, penalties excluded. A lot of that success is down to him. He lives and breathes football 24 hours a day. At City, he wanted to be involved much more than he was, but here at Arsenal, he's at the very heart of what we do. There's barely a training session that doesn't feature at least some set-piece work.

As soon as we get a corner, a free kick or even a throw-in within the final third, you see him jump up and shout to us from the coaching zone. He sees things us players don't see or might not find that important. He comes up with intricate choreographies and new ideas all the time. If one day I become a manager, I will seek out somebody like Nico for my staff. Any team competing at the highest level needs a set-piece specialist as brilliant as he is.

After Dubai, you could see the freshness return in an unbeaten run of 11 games in the league that was sprinkled with huge wins, including a 3-1 over Liverpool that gave us real momentum in the title race. Unfortunately, my right calf muscle, a weak spot of mine, closed up completely a few minutes into the game against Jürgen Klopp's men. After my mistake against Salah in the first game, there was no way I was coming off that early. But I could barely run by half-time and needed to be subbed. I missed the next four weeks, including a series of big results against West Ham (6-0), Burnley (5-0), Newcastle United (4-1) and Sheffield United (6-0).

Not being able to play really affects my mental well-being. I want to be on the pitch. I want to be with the team, helping them win games. When I'm playing football, I'm a happy man. And when I'm happy, I'm bringing all these positive emotions home to my family. But not being fit is worse than losing. You're frustrated that your body has let you down. And you feel sorry for letting the team down, even though there's nothing you can do about it. As much as you want to keep those negative feelings outside the house, they follow you inside and cling to you like a bad smell. You try to hide it as much as you can, but the kids pick up on it. And then you feel even worse and guilty for affecting the mood.

Vlada gets caught up in it all as well. She's totally involved in my football life and tries to see all the games. I think she loves football more than me, even. She's always asking me questions about how things are going; she's always on it. That's why, when I'm injured, she feels even worse than me, which in turn makes me feel sad too.

Picking up repeat injuries is a scary thing for a footballer. I've had problems with my right calf for a couple of years now. We've been investigating the reasons and might have some ideas how to avoid problems in the future. What people don't realise is that you have to work a lot harder, three or four times as much, when you're injured, compared with your team-mates. They will train a couple of hours and then go home, and after games they'll have a day off. Injured players will do physio four to five hours a day, every day of the week. Some people might think, 'Oh, he's off and enjoying another holiday,' but it's the opposite, in terms of workload and mindset. When you're injured, it's much harder to switch off because you're constantly thinking about getting fit again and worry if it's taking longer than anticipated.

I came back from injury but was no longer a regular starter. Mikel and the coaching staff tried everything to help me, as did the other players. That's not a given. I've seen it in other clubs; you can be completely on your own, with nobody paying you much attention. It's much, much better this way. Before the Luton game on 3 April, the boss took me aside and gave me a USB stick, a 'best of' with my finest moments in an Arsenal shirt to motivate me and remind me that I'm a good player. I really felt that he was with me in that moment. He clearly wanted to help me, offering his support to get the best out of me. Unfortunately, I wasn't able to repay his faith.

I didn't start the Champions League game against Bayern at home but came on at half-time. We drew 2-2. Not great, but an okay performance. But then came Aston Villa, a 2-0 home defeat that all but buried our title ambitions. A few days later, we were knocked out by Bayern. Within the space of a week, our trophy ambitions had taken a serious knock.

The pressure was becoming greater and greater at the time, but I didn't see that being a factor. We had very broad shoulders in the dressing room. I don't believe those defeats had anything to do with that. People always look for narratives, stories that make sense of a game that doesn't always follow logic. They look for a pattern, for explanations. Over the course of a full campaign, there are clear reasons for things working or not working. But a couple of matches can always go against you without you knowing why. We should have done better, that's all.

The Bayern games were very edgy. No side created many chances. They took one more than us. I don't think it's deeper than that. Villa was a pretty 'dead' game. Not a lot was happening. They were really patient, as they knew we were chasing the title and had to come at them. Their target was not to concede the first goal. The value of the first goal is huge in the Premier League. When you score first, the other team opens up a bit. We had a couple of good chances we didn't take. It could have been a different story. But Villa punished us.

And: I was awful. I was my worst enemy in that game.

You might say, everyone had a pretty poor game against Villa. But I'm not everyone. I had a terrible game, and can't hide behind the fact that others didn't play to their potential either. If anything, that's when you need to step up even more as an experienced pro. It's easy to just go with the flow when everyone's flying. You also need to turn up in games when the team struggles. That game effectively killed off the season for us. And afterwards, I was dropped for good. I didn't start another game until the end of the season.

In all honesty, it wasn't the greatest year for me personally. Injuries didn't help, but that can't be an excuse. I still played quite a few games and should have done better. If you're on the pitch, you're fit to play. And if you're fit to play, you need to be at your best. I made far too many silly mistakes on the ball. I feel ashamed about it. It wasn't good enough, not even close. It's not because I have such high expectations of myself that I cannot meet them. Not at all. But I can't drop below my base level. In too many games, I did.

I know what I have to do on the pitch. The coaching staff, the manager, the players, too, all tell me the same thing: 'Alex, your best quality is to play simple football. Just pass the ball. Pass, pass, pass.' When you do that, your confidence goes up another level. You're starting to be super, super confident. That's the stage you start to make silly mistakes. I know I'm prone to that. People who know me well can see it in little things like my body language: 'Oh, he looks overconfident.' Most players will get things wrong when they lack confidence. For me, it's more likely to be the other way around. That's the trigger for me. Then I try to overcomplicate things and turn something simple into something special. That's always a mistake. I was guilty of that a lot.

I used to only pick up on that after games, but I can recognise it now while it's happening and snap out of it better. I'm aware of this unfortunate tendency of mine and try to clamp down on it. You never stop trying to improve in this game. Defensively, I was exposed a couple of times as well. A lot of people blamed me for it, and I have to take responsibility. I'm the first one to criticise myself. But not all goals were entirely preventable.

It's a bit tricky when there's a mismatch between your own performances and that of the team. Arsenal had a pretty good campaign, all told, with some stellar individual performances. Martin, Bukayo, our two centre-backs, Ben White, David Raya…They all had a fantastic season. The squad has a real nice depth to it now. When everyone's fit, you look at the bench and see so much quality in every position. Fighting for every trophy possible, you need to have this wealth of talent, otherwise you won't last the distance. But personally, I wasn't anywhere near my usual level. You see all those happy faces around you and you're either not involved at all or play well below the standards you've set yourself. It hurts. You feel guilty.

Your duty as a player is to support your team at all times irrespective of your state of mind, though. It can't be an ego trip. If they're playing better than you, take it as a positive: that's your reference, an example of the levels you need to get back to in order to deserve your position in the squad. In fact, you need to push yourself even further than that. The aim is to try to be better than your team-mates. You will have to be, in case there's strong competition for places, and two or three players are fighting for the same position. You push each other every single day on the training sessions and in the games.

True team-mates will support you. They'll come up to you before the game for a hug and offer words of encouragement. If you're lacking focus during the game, they will scream at you to wake up. It doesn't mean they think you're a bad player. They're just trying to help you. You need to take these moments in the spirit that they're intended. I do the same. If I see a player doing silly things on the pitch or having the wrong attitude, I will push him. I will scream at him.

People got very excited when Ben White and I had a bit of a 'ding dong', as they say in England, a misunderstanding that turned into a bit of an argument after our 2-1 win at Nottingham Forest in January. But honestly, there was no problem at all. It never got personal. These things happen a million times a season. It's just a usual day at the office, the difference being that in this particular moment, millions of people can see you speak with your fellow co-worker. Afterwards, we had another really good conversation and it was all over in a flash. Zero resentment, no bad feelings whatsoever.

The Mister told reporters a few days later that Ben and I lived in the same house and shared wives. I can confirm that neither is true. He said it for a laugh, of course, but he also wanted to convey a more serious message. 'You don't argue with someone if you don't have a great relationship,' he said. 'That happens because you have the trust and chemistry with somebody, to react the way they did.'

He is spot-on. Having players shouting at each other on the pitch is not a sign of discord but unity. We're helping each other, correcting each other's mistakes. That's how it should be. The more I see it at Arsenal, the happier I am. As long as that's happening, you're making progress as a team. One day, if I'm a manager, I want my team coaching themselves as much as possible on the training ground and in matches. That's how they will develop an understanding to play in certain situations with their eyes closed. I'm not ready for managing just yet, though; it will be a while. In the meantime, I want to do my best as a footballer. Accepting help from your team-mates without taking it personally or badly is a big part of it, and I expect the same of them.

Being an Arsenal player, there's another thing I grasped last season. It's a good lesson for any young player reading this. If you have the opportunity of playing every game as a regular, don't think it'll always be like that. Because one day, after a couple of bad games or even one poor performance, you can get dropped in a flash. And earning your place back is tough. Super tough. It's a punch in the gut, where it really hurts. Those who manage these kinds of inevitable disappointments well, adopting the right attitude, will succeed. That's one of the biggest challenges in football.

But many players react the exact opposite way. I've seen it a lot in the past. I used to do it myself as well; my attitude was not always good in training sessions. And then, at the end of the day, you come back home, and you're just talking to yourself angrily, wondering why you went to the training ground with a bad face and didn't give your best. Who was helped by that? Who was I trying to show that I'm not happy? I just made things worse for myself. You're not going to get far in a team sport with this kind of egocentric attitude, no matter how good you are as a player.

The natural reaction is to blame others. That happens a lot in football, but not just in football. It's always someone else's fault, never your own. Blame yourself instead. Look for the flaws in your game. But be careful not to undermine yourself. Don't question your ability too much. You need to know the limits. Find the balance, the golden middle. And try to avoid emotions. Work on your mindset. I saw guys go off the rails in these situations at other clubs. They were sulking and radiated negative energy. Nobody wants that.

A lot of experienced players used to tell me, 'Alex, one session can change your life.' And it's true. You can have a bad training session, fight with someone on the coaching staff, and then, regardless of who's right or wrong, you're gone. Not immediately. But little by little, you're going down, until you find yourself at a much smaller club. I've seen it with my own eyes.

That's why consistency is one of the best qualities any footballer can have. Consistency in performance and attitude. Same output and input every single day. It's bloody hard. But that's what separates the best players from the rest. I decided for myself a while ago that I would always find the positive in everything, even when I was being dropped. I treat it as a challenge, as a chance for growth. To be able to give your best every single day, and stay positive, come what may, is one of the most difficult things in professional football. But if you can do that, it shows that you are strong enough mentally. That's the basis for success.

Football can be a cruel game but it's also amazing. Why? Because it will always give you another opportunity to come back from disappointment. Take it from someone who's spent big chunks of his career being written off at the start of every season.

Okay, you have a bad day at the office. Start from tomorrow. Start again. Prove yourself again to the manager, to the coaching staff, and to yourself. You can do it. Just start to be focused on every single action during the training session, every single second. Have standards for yourself. Don't lose silly balls, be focused, be full of energy. Immerse yourself fully in those moments, be present with everything you've got. It's only one hour or one and a half hours of the day of training. Use that time well.

At the end of March, we drew 0-0 at Manchester City to become the first team in nearly 900 days to leave the Etihad with a clean sheet. That match and the Villa defeat aside, we won every one of our last 18 league games. No one could accuse us of mental frailty in the run-in this time. The longer the campaign went on, the more solid we became.

Before the final match of the season, at home to Everton, we spoke about the fact that one more win and a total of 89 points would still not be enough if City won their match against West Ham. I don't want to spoil the surprise, but they did. We were all disappointed there was no happy ending on the final day of the campaign, but there was also immense pride. Eighty-nine points is a crazy number, the second-best record in Arsenal's Premier League history, just one point off Arsène Wenger's Invincibles from 2003-04. The Mister was right to call it an historic achievement.

We set a club record of 28 wins in the Premier League. We didn't lose a game in any matches against the other big six sides. We had the best defensive record. We had 19 clean sheets, by far the best defence in the league. We scored 91 goals, another club record in the Premier League era.

We can – and must – look at all the silly points we dropped and try to improve. But we shouldn't be too harsh on ourselves, because we were up against one of the most extraordinary sides football has ever seen. This City team are something else. I saw people question their hunger after winning the treble. They said they're not quite good enough this season, that they were vulnerable. I was hoping and praying that they were right, that they would drop points on the last day of the season and give us a chance to win the league, but in my heart of hearts, I knew it was unlikely. Just look at the numbers. They dominated every single game they were playing. The way they control situations, it's super hard to hurt them.

City do it so well. They're so patient, they never rush things. They probe away, looking for openings with 50, 70 passes. We're on our way to being as good as they are, I'm certain of that. I don't want us to copy City, and Mikel doesn't want to either. Different players will make for different styles. But City show you how to dominate an opponent completely, how you will always have more of the ball. We want that as well. And we are growing as a team all the time; we're becoming more mature. You can feel we are getting closer to the benchmark they've set. They're pushing us, and it's a pleasure to be up against this kind of competition. If you want to be the best, you need to beat the best. Simple.

We need to learn from their consistency and their attitude, even on our holidays. In the off-season, I went to the south of France. I saw on Instagram that Bernardo Silva was there as well. I texted him, asking if he knew a pitch to do some exercises. From his time playing at Monaco, he knows the area well. He wrote back saying, 'For what do you need a pitch?' 'I need to run,' I replied.

He wrote back: 'Run? For what? You're going to try to win the Premier League again? Forget about it. Stay at home.' I bumped into their Belgian winger, Jérémy Doku, a few days later and showed him the chat. He was laughing his head off. We've been pushing each other for two seasons already. That experience will make us stronger.

You can see how far we've already come by the way teams play against us. They increasingly sit deep, afraid of leaving open spaces. Nottingham Forest had 11 players inside their box in the first half. What we need to learn is a bit of patience. We don't need to rush. The Mister put it well: 'I want to drive 100 mph but I can't if I have three buses and 55 taxis ahead of me.' We need to move teams from one side to the other, three or four times, until we catch them out and bite them. This is one of the things we will have to develop further, because we're going to have more games like that next season.

My personal priority will be to stay fit. When you're fit, you are important for the team. When you're injured, you're not important and no one really cares about you.

That sounds brutal, but that's the reality. And I have to prove that I really deserve to be part of the Arsenal starting XI once more. I already know that I am good enough, I just need to show it again. I've been around long enough to know how this goes. Be patient, work hard. Start from the basics, get them right on the pitch. Be confident in yourself, believe in yourself and your ability. Who can stop you then? No one. If you do all of that with the right attitude, you will give the manager a big headache. That's for sure.

I'm also certain our supporters have plenty of reasons to feel excited about the next few years. Arsenal have an unbelievable future ahead of us with all these young players in the squad. And we certainly have the right manager in Mikel. In my time in football, I have never seen anyone work this hard as he and his staff do every single day, to cover all the details, all the eventualities.

He put a big emphasis on taking 'the Emirates factor' into away games. The club put up photos of the players, posters and banners in the changing rooms. One of them that was picked up by social media read, 'BASICS' – Boxes, Attack, Shape, Intensity, Compete and Set pieces. We had it up in the Tottenham Hotspur changing room for our 3-2 win there in April. The Mister even brought a replica of our famous stadium clock to matches. The idea was that players should feel more at home, more relaxed. On a subconscious level, he also sent a very smart message: this was our place.

He pays attention to everything. Somebody at the club told me that he watches clips from opposition managers' pre-match conferences, scanning for clues about the line-up and tactics, and that he also studies footage of the other team arriving at the ground. He also likes to play little games with the opposition. I've seen him tell injured players to come on the team bus and walk into the dressing room with their wash bag, to put the other manager off the scent. Everything he does is geared towards finding an edge and fostering a spirit of community. We had a big barbecue at the training ground in a repeat of the get-together from Dubai. It went down really well.

And we must mention Win as well. Win is a chocolate Labrador, a therapy dog who lives at the training ground. The Mister chose her personally. She joined us at the end of the 2022-23 season and is beloved by everyone. She's so kind. You just want to hug her in the morning. Everyone's happy to see her. Players look after her along with a member of the staff, and they have taken her home to spend time with their kids as well. She's so gentle. And everyone feels responsible for her. Mikel's idea was to foster that family feeling and bring everyone together in their shared fondness for Win. And for winning, I guess. Our lives are shaped by what we love.

A club working so smartly, at this pace, will find success for sure. And the team, still young and gaining in knowledge, will get better at dealing with sticky situations along the way.

I don't think it's brave to predict we will be one of the favourites in any competition we take part in. I am 100 per cent sure we are on the right track, the way we all work together, help each other, push each other. We will be able to make our supporters happy by lifting trophies in due course. That's what they really want to see. And that's no less than they deserve, for giving us such massive support.

15

Believe

After the disappointment of not making it to the World Cup, Ukraine were even more determined to qualify for the Euros in Germany. It would be the perfect stage for reminding everyone of our fight for survival and for providing at least a bit of temporary relief from the horrors of war.

The draw wasn't exactly kind to us. We were pitted against Italy and England, the two finalists from Euro 2020, in our qualification group. First game: Wembley, 26 March 2023. Seeing the Ukrainian flags fly on Wembley Way was very touching. The atmosphere inside the ground felt more like a friendly, with Ukrainian colours everywhere. 'This is more than just a football game for us,' Andriy Shevchenko told the crowd before kick-off. 'People are fighting for the right to exist.'

The FA had invited 1,000 refugees and their families. Many more turned out to support us. Even some of the locals were cheering us on. 'This is the first time I've not wanted England to win,' Steven Gerrard said. I don't think I have ever experienced an international game quite like this. You could really feel the love for Ukraine. England were too strong for us, though. We lost 2-0. In the return match in Wrocław, we dug deep to get a 1-1 draw. But a somewhat controversial 0-0 with Italy – we had a big penalty shout turned down late on – in the last game in Leverkusen, forced us to contest the play-offs.

We were five minutes from abject failure, trailing Bosnia and Herzegovina 1-0, but scored two goals in three minutes to snatch a win. Getting knocked out at this stage didn't bear thinking about. I don't think we could have shown our faces back home. We were so relieved we turned it around right at the end. There's nothing like coming back from behind late on in a football game. But when that happens in the middle of a war, with a whole nation looking to you to bring a bit of happiness and hope, it's a million times bigger. We were still here. Still alive.

Iceland, again at Wrocław, was the final hurdle. We went down 1-0 once more. I wasn't fully fit but was able to come on and help the team win 2-1 a second time. We had done it! Without home advantage. With players who had their lives turned upside down. I felt so proud to be Ukrainian in that moment, but I could hardly celebrate after the final whistle. I had left all my emotions out on the pitch. I was totally exhausted but beyond happy, too.

Germany, here we come.

Before I headed to the tournament, Vlada and I went back to Ukraine with the family (minus Louie and Mia) for the christening of Leia, our second child. I was invited to attend a big event from United24, where they presented all the projects they have been working on for the last two years.

In addition to the rebuild of the school, I took on another urgent case they're working on. Sashko, 11, and Artur, eight, are two football-crazy boys from Bakhmut. Their home, like the rest of the city, was totally destroyed by the Russians. Their family had to flee twice and ended up in Kyiv. Father, mother, the boys and the grandparents, six people sleeping in one room, taking turns to sleep in one bed. They're staying near the academy of Lokomotyv Kyiv, whose stadium was damaged by a missile. The hall housing the futsal pitch was destroyed.

United24 put me in touch with Nova Poshta, a big media group, and we decided we would do something for these kids. I could really see myself in them, dreaming of making it as a footballer, and their story touched me. The people from United24 showed me a video of Sashko playing football in a bombed street, wearing my shirt. I really wanted to get involved and make a difference. We bought them an apartment. I met the family on the pretence of wanting a bit of a kickaround with the boys and gifting them signed shirts, but luckily, we were able to make a more meaningful impact on their lives. We were all in tears when I told them the news.

I said to the boys, 'You can lose your house and the life you used to live, but you cannot lose the dream in your heart. If you're going to work hard to achieve it, you will achieve it.' It's far too early to know if either of them will make it as a player, but that's not really important. I just really wanted to help this family, help them to hold on to their dreams amid all this chaos and deprivation.

There are thousands of cases like this in Ukraine. I'm not a fan of making a big song and dance of helping people on social media or in a book like this. That's not me. But someone much smarter than me who works at United24 told me: 'You are not doing this to show off. Only silly people will see it this way. You are posting this because you want to draw attention to this work and get others to get involved as well. Don't worry about negative reactions from haters.' And you know what? I don't care any more. Some will say I'm talking about these things to build up my profile. But you can't be loved by everyone. There will be enough people who will understand. I'm hoping that a few of them might feel moved to chip in as well, maybe more, maybe less than me, it doesn't matter. Any help makes a big difference on the ground.

On the eve of the tournament, the federation released a video with me and 12 other national team players whose home towns were damaged or occupied by Russian forces. We wanted to show the world what war means. As representatives of our nation, there was no use pretending the Euros were about only football for us. Being in the heart of Europe, part of the European family of nations, was in itself a powerful message. The location of our base camp in Taunusstein, not far outside Frankfurt, also had a symbolic dimension. We were close to the headquarters of the US Army in Germany, from where the shipment of arms to Ukraine is being coordinated. President Zelensky had visited there six months earlier. There was a heavy security detail for us. Every time we left the hotel, a police helicopter watched over us from above.

'The more we talk about the war, the better for us to deal with it,' our national team manager, Serhiy Rebrov, said after the first training session. It was an open event with more than 4,000 supporters in the Wehen Wiesbaden Arena, many of them refugees or soldiers receiving medical treatment there. Germany has taken in 1.3 million Ukrainians since February 2022. Each player presented one ball to a fan. When my turn came, I met a veteran who had lost both legs beneath the knee in defence of our country. It was one of those truly humbling moments that brought home how small our role is in comparison with the bravery of those at the sharp end.

An opera singer sang the national anthem. There were speeches by local politicians that pledged their support for us and the whole of Ukraine. The mood was similar to the one at Stamford Bridge during the Game4Ukraine, a celebration of unity, defiance and loyalty.

Everything went really well. But then came the opening game against Romania in Munich.

The ball doesn't know whether your team is playing for a just cause. It doesn't care about the colours on your shirt. If you don't treat it well, it will punish you without a moment's hesitation. That's what happened to us. From the first second, you could feel that we weren't quite in it. We lost too many duels, we weren't aggressive enough to create more chances up front. Every footballer who's ever played this game knows you have those games when, for whatever reason, you're not quite as sharp as your opponent. You look for reasons, that's how the human psyche works. But having thought about this for many weeks now, I still can't give you a good explanation.

Did we underestimate the Romanians? One hundred per cent not. We were all aware how good they were on the ball and that winning this game was key for further progress at this competition. Was the pressure too much? I can't speak for everyone, only myself, but again, I don't think so. It's up to you to accept this situation and take it either as extra motivation or as extra pressure, and handle it in the right way. Big pressure, little pressure, no pressure – as soon as you step on the pitch, you just need to be focused on your team, what needs to be done, and show the desire to win. And that's exactly what we missed.

We just didn't do enough off and on the ball. I can't tell you why; I can only tell you that it happened. I, for example, should have done a lot more going forward. Go on overlaps beyond the wide midfielder to get behind the opposition defence. Play better passes. We had a degree of control but never hurt them. We were too safe. Talking among the players and with the national manager afterwards, we all came to the same conclusion: we needed to show more hunger, get stuck in more. Simple, but hard to do sometimes.

Losing 3-0 was the worst of two worlds. If you must lose your opening game, try to keep the score down to give yourself a chance in the next two games. The way the format works, four third-placed teams were going through to the knockouts, which is why goal difference was very important. But we had messed that up as well. We were totally up against it now.

The next day, I saw Georgia play against Turkey. They lost 3-1 in their first-ever game in this competition, but they really went for it. It was a crazy game, up and down, with many chances on either side. Georgia were unlucky they didn't get anything from that match. As a supporter, I would have been proud of my team, despite the result. They had shown heart, courage, effort. We looked at that game and understood where we had fallen short. If we had shown only 50 per cent of Georgia's commitment, we would never have lost 3-0.

Things started badly against Slovakia, too. We were 1-0 down after 17 minutes. But the attitude was much better. It's the little things. High-fives after winning tackles. Celebrating throw-ins. We were really fighting for each other, especially in the second half. I didn't see that against Romania. We won 2-1. Our position was still difficult because of the poor goal difference, but we were still in it. The mood was much better. We were sure we could do some damage against Belgium, and we knew a win would take us through to the last 16.

I didn't play one good pass or win a single tackle in the first 60 minutes of the Belgium game. But for once, that wasn't my fault. The manager hadn't picked me for the starting XI. I was surprised but accepted it. I decided a long time ago that I would always respect a manager's decision because they always do what they think is best for the team. There is no agenda. I will never complain, only work harder.

Watching from the sidelines, I thought we could win. The Belgians played for the draw, which is always a difficult thing to do. We had a couple of chances. I came on in the second half to try to find a goal. In the last 15-20 minutes, I played everywhere. A draw between Romania and Slovakia meant we needed three points to make it out of the group. We tried our best but couldn't force the one goal that would have made all the difference.

The dressing room was heavy with sadness and regret afterwards. We had four points, which would have been enough to go through in any other group. But because of that horror show from the first game, we were only in fourth spot and went home. We had failed. The plan, at a minimum, was to qualify for the next stage and go as far as we can. But we fell at the first hurdle. It was a shock for us, but also a good lesson. You cannot start a competition the way we did. We will try to learn from it for the World Cup in 2026.

This wasn't just a sporting defeat for us. I feel that we let our country down. We were disappointed in us, for disappointing millions of Ukraine supporters back home and all around the world. It hurt us players the most. I don't know if it's necessary to apologise to all our fans, because it's already happened and we must move on. But I do want them to know we all feel sorry we couldn't match the incredible spirit our country has shown on the pitches in Germany. We should have given a better account of ourselves.

Failure on such an important stage for the whole of Ukraine can take you to dark places. For me, this body blow brought back the uncomfortable questions I have been asking myself since the war began. Am I doing enough? Is playing football the right thing to do while my country burns and children are killed in their hospital beds by Russian missiles? Shouldn't I be there?

But on the balance, when you reflect a little bit and the raw pain of the disappointment resides, the answers are still the same. Being a professional outside Ukraine is an unbelievable privilege that comes with the moral duty to speak out, bang the drum as loud as I can and do anything in my power to support our real heroes – those who are fighting at the front, the volunteers and people on the ground.

One day, when my daughters are older, they will ask me, 'Daddy, what did you do during the war in our country? How much did you help the people?' I just want to look into their eyes and say, 'Well, me and your mum, we tried to do our best.'

We have often talked among ourselves in the national team about this subject. Will there be a time when we will all have to go and fight? I'm thinking about my wife having to live without a husband and my kids without a dad. Who will be next? After us, it will be our kids. And there won't be a country at all any more eventually. That's what Russia is trying to achieve.

If I'm being totally honest with myself, I do feel guilty sometimes, knowing that hundreds of thousands of people are fighting while I'm in London, going to training at Colney or playing in matches. But that guilt drives you to make a difference. Whenever you feel you are helping, the guilt goes away, if only for a fleeting moment. But then there's another guilt. You feel guilty about not doing more. My wife tries to go to Ukraine as much as she can; she feels very bad about not being there. Her dream is to move back as soon as possible. She understands, of course, that I have a job, that I have a contract, that I still want to play at the highest level, as long as I can.

Eventually, I really want to live in Ukraine again, too. It's the best place for me, the place where I feel myself. I might go into coaching, I don't know yet. But after football, we will go back there, to have a rest and a break from the game, and to have a normal life. I really hope the war will be over by that stage, but nobody knows. I'm worried that we're going to fight it for many more years. I don't think even the people in charge know what's next. All I can see, from the outside, is that the situation is getting tougher for us all the time. I don't see a solution, unfortunately.

As the president of Ukraine, you might say, 'A lot of people on both sides have been killed. Those who haven't been killed are tired of the war. There's been so much destruction. We need to negotiate. Maybe we can come to an agreement. You keep the land that you occupy and leave us alone.' How would Ukrainians react to that? Each of them has two or three people in their circle who were killed, injured, raped or had to flee their homes. They have defended our independence, our homes, our piece of land. And then you have the president sign away our land to those terrorists? How would you feel about that if your son, brother or father has fought for two and a half years? They will say, 'Why didn't we give them this land before?' And in the meantime, those who live in the occupied territories will continue to be terrorised, sent to camps, made to be Russians or killed. People think soldiers not shooting on the battlefront equals peace, but it doesn't. For those who find themselves under Russian occupation, the suffering continues. I understand little about politics, but I think any Ukrainian president will find it incredibly hard to agree to such a deal.

I remember a TV interview with Putin. He said, 'The Ukrainian government are stupid. They could have finished this war ages ago, but they don't even speak with us.' And so on. How can you sit down and speak to the guy who's responsible for the killing and rape of so many people, and the guy who wants to take part of your land and make it his? But let's say we do negotiate. We will lose these territories forever and promise to stay out of

NATO, and in turn they will promise to leave us alone. How much is that promise worth? In 1994, we surrendered our nuclear weapons to Russia and they said they would recognise our independence and the sovereignty of our borders, that they would protect us from any attacks. We know how that one worked out.

The whole world respected our independence – apart from one country whose leader got up one day in the morning and thought, 'I want to conquer this land.' So with whom, exactly, would you like us to negotiate or sign a peace treaty? A deal might stop the war for two, three or maybe five years, but they will go again after that, trying to cut off another slice of the cake. They will replenish their weapons, refresh their army and then attack once more. To them, human lives are nothing. Even their own soldiers are not people to them, just meat for the grinder.

I don't see how you can sign a peace treaty when you don't have a partner willing to respect it. Our president understands you cannot come to an agreement with them. At the same time, more and more people on our side are dying each day. The economy is really suffering. When everyone is fighting, what will be left of our country? Zelensky is in an impossible spot. When I sometimes think about this dilemma and how tough it must be for him, my head wants to explode.

The truth is, we have no choice but to fight on right now. We cannot just give up, raise our hands and say, 'We're too fatigued to carry on, just do anything you want.' The price we would pay for that is too high. And it wouldn't stop with us. Look at the map: Ukraine is a shield for Europe. If we break, they will continue and get into more countries. Then the war will not just be on your television screens but at your doorstep. I don't wish that on anyone. But it's important to understand what's at stake here. The whole free world must see to it that Ukraine prevails. If these terrorists are allowed to get away with it – simply invading another country, killing thousands and chopping off bits of land without any major repercussions – others will be encouraged to do the same.

We all have to believe we will win. You have to try to find the optimism in anything, because what's the point of living if you're a pessimist? All of us hope this nightmare will finish soon. But while this is going on, we will have to protect our families and our homes any which way we can. When the war started, many said Ukraine wouldn't last a month. But we're still here. We have shown our soul to the world.

I would like to thank everyone in the world who has helped us help ourselves so far. But this is not over. We are still fighting, and we still need help. If you are able to, please support us, either by donating to Ukraine or by putting pressure on your government to send us weapons. Don't switch off. Don't leave us alone in the dark in this desperate hour of need. Don't give up on us. We would rather die than give up. That spirit of freedom will bring us victory. But we cannot do it alone.

ACKNOWLEDGEMENTS

I'd like to thank Raphael Honigstein for helping me to write this book. He's done an incredible job.

My thanks also go to Arti Rjabovs for connecting us, to David Luxton, to my publisher Ian Marshall and the whole wonderful team at Bloomsbury.

I owe a huge debt of gratitude to Andriy Shevchenko, the players, coaches and everyone involved with organising Game4Ukraine.

Spending time with the tireless staff of United24, I have been exposed to many horrors but also to the powerful impact of direct help on the ground. There is so much more that can and must be done to help the people of Ukraine make it through this devastating war. Please visit www.u24.gov.ua to support them in this monumental effort. Thank you.

IMAGE CREDITS

Orthodox Christmas: courtesy of the author
Pet budgerigar: courtesy of the author
Early football medal: courtesy of the author
School photo: courtesy of the author
Challenging Héctor Bellerín: David Price/Arsenal FC via Getty Images
First international goal: Marco Bertorello/AFP via Getty Images
Vlada at Euro 2016: courtesy of the author
On loan at PSV Eindhoven: VI Images via Getty Images
Champions League debut: A. Hassenstein/FC Bayern via Getty Images
With Phillip Cocu: VI Images via Getty Images
First game for Manchester City: Gareth Copley/Getty Images
Celebrating first Premier League win: courtesy of the author
Champions League match against Shakhtar Donetsk: Clive Brunskill/Getty Images
With Pep Guardiola: Visionhaus/Getty Images
Mistake against Southampton: Glyn Kirk/AFP via Getty Images
With Vincent Kompany: James Williamson - AMA/Getty Images
With Anatoliy Patuk: courtesy of the author
Against Mo Salah: Andrew Powell/Liverpool FC via Getty Images
Engagement to Vlada: courtesy of the author

IMAGE CREDITS

Friendly against Cyprus: Stanislav Vedmid/DeFodi Images via Getty Images
Scoring against Sweden in Euro 2020: Ross Parker/SNS Group via Getty Images
Playing against Peterborough in the week of Russia's invasion: James Williamson - AMA/Getty Images
Ukraine flag around Premier League trophy: Stu Forster/Getty Images
With Vlada, Eva and trophy: Simon Stacpoole/Offside/Offside via Getty Images
Press conference: Andy Buchanan/AFP via Getty Images
Singing the Ukrainian national anthem: Mark Runnacles/Getty Images
Signing with Arsenal: Stuart MacFarlane/Arsenal FC via Getty Images
Beating Spurs at Tottenham Hotspur stadium: Marc Atkins/Getty Images
Beating Manchester United in stoppage time: Ash Donelon/Manchester United via Getty Images
With Mikel Arteta: David Price/Arsenal FC via Getty Images
Captaining on the one-year anniversary of invasion: Darren Staples/AFP via Getty Images
With Andriy Shevchenko: courtesy of United24
With Arsène Wenger: Justin Tallis/AFP via Getty Images
With Kai Havertz: Mike Hewitt/Getty Images
Our dogs: courtesy of the author
Family photo: courtesy of the author
With Artem Dovbyk: Sergei Gapon/AFP via Getty Images
Playing Slovakia in Euro 2024: Jan Fromme - firo sportphoto/Getty Images
For Ukraine: Matt McNulty - UEFA/UEFA via Getty Images

A NOTE ON THE AUTHOR

Born in Radomyshl, Oleksandr Zinchenko was thirteen years old when he joined the academy of Shakhtar Donetsk, Ukraine's most successful football club. Zinchenko went on to join Manchester City in 2016. A versatile player, he started his career as an attacking midfielder, but eventually converted into a left-back or wing-back under Pep Guardiola, winning nine major honours at the club. He joined Arsenal in the summer of 2022, and by the start of 2024–25 he had won 66 caps for Ukraine.

A NOTE ON THE TYPE

The text of this book is set in Fournier. Fournier is derived from the *romain du roi*, which was created towards the end of the seventeenth century from designs made by a committee of the Académie of Sciences for the exclusive use of the Imprimerie Royale. The original Fournier types were cut by the famous Paris founder Pierre Simon Fournier in about 1742. These types were some of the most influential designs of the eight and are counted among the earliest examples of the 'transitional' style of typeface. This Monotype version dates from 1924. Fournier is a light, clear face whose distinctive features are capital letters that are quite tall and bold in relation to the lowercase letters, and *decorative italics*, which show the influence of the calligraphy of Fournier's time.